# The Consolations of God

## GREAT SERMONS
## OF PHILLIPS BROOKS

# The Consolations of God

## GREAT SERMONS
## OF PHILLIPS BROOKS

*Edited by*

Ellen Wilbur

WILLIAM B. EERDMANS PUBLISHING COMPANY
GRAND RAPIDS, MICHIGAN / CAMBRIDGE, U.K.

*I would like to thank Heather Cole and Christie Wilbur for use of Harvard's libraries, as well as Christopher Wilbur, Pamela Post, and all others kind enough to read and respond to certain of Brooks' sermons. Also, I'd like to thank Tatiana Winger for her help, and Daniel Aaron, Justin Kaplan, and Samuel Lloyd for their encouragement and/or advice.*

Wm. B. Eerdmans Publishing Co.
255 Jefferson Ave. S.E., Grand Rapids, Michigan 49503 /
P.O. Box 163, Cambridge CB3 9PU U.K.

Printed in the United States of America

08 07 06 05 04 03    7 6 5 4 3 2 1

**Library of Congress Cataloging-in-Publication Data**

Brooks, Phillips, 1835-1893.
The consolations of God: great sermons of Phillips Brooks /
edited by Ellen Wilbur.
p.    cm.
ISBN 0-8028-1353-4 (pbk.: alk. paper)
1. Sermon, American — 19th century. 2. Episcopal Church — Sermons.
I. Wilbur, Ellen. II. Title.
BX5937.B83C66  2003

252'.03 — dc21

2003052853

www.eerdmans.com

*In Memory of Phillips Brooks*

# Contents

—◠—

# *Foreword*

—⚏—

On nearly every Sunday for more than thirty years, I have had the great duty and honor of standing in a pulpit in Harvard University that is dedicated to the memory of Phillips Brooks, a graduate of Harvard College. A gift of the Vestry of Trinity Church, Boston, in memory of its great rector, the pulpit has served both to inspire and to intimidate every preacher who, since its installation in 1932, has had the privilege of preaching from it.

I, for one, pray that the spirit that was evident in Brooks and so animated his preaching might from time to time abide in those of us who stand in his stead, and I am sure that the good rectors of Trinity Church who succeeded him have often prayed the same. There is something reassuring about standing in places where Brooks performed so well that which by our own lights we try to do; and thus, on behalf of all of us who preach and who take pleasure in preaching, I have the honor of introducing this new volume of the sermons of Phillips Brooks.

Ellen Wilbur has done a great and good service in preparing a volume of Brooks' sermons, for she has rescued from obscurity one who was always destined to be our contemporary. In bringing these sermons to light for another generation and century, she allows us the benefit of one of the truly great preachers of the American and Christian experience.

Preaching is an ephemeral thing, potent at the moment of impact but, like snow, soon gone. Preaching is preserved first in the minds and hearts of those who hear it, for it is a medium meant to be heard, but then its only future is in the unnatural medium of print, where that which is heard is often different in affect from that which is read. Rare is the preacher whose words survive the transition from ear to eye; fortunately for us, Phillips Brooks was such a preacher. In his day Brooks enjoyed a celebrity status that we would now attribute to a rock or media star whose image is invented and maintained by a host of flacks; in the last third of the nineteenth century the name of Phillips Brooks was synonymous with the very best of a popular medium. It would help to remember that preaching used to be a form of popular entertainment, with the preacher at the apex of public life, and that even though it is hard for us in this wordy but inarticulate age to understand the powerful public appeal of preaching, the appeal was not solely moral or religious. Preaching was public discourse, a source of mental and moral stimulation, and for the most part it was free of charge. The habit of "sermon tasting" was deeply ingrained in the culture, and urban churches in particular were known not so much by their liturgy, music, or architecture as by their preacher.

In late Victorian Boston, the brightest star in a galaxy of shining homiletical stars was Phillips Brooks of Trinity Church. People from his own parish and from the growing suburbs and beyond flocked to hear him, and he was considered one of the "must-sees" in Boston for the growing tourist industry, along with the State House, Faneuil Hall, and Boston Common. The new Trinity Church, built to Brooks' taste by the great architect Henry Hobson Richardson, his friend and collaborator, was essentially a stage setting for Brooks, with the massive Romanesque scale of the building — perhaps the most significant religious edifice in America — designed to accommodate the massive physical scale of Brooks himself. He was in every sense a large man, well over six feet tall and of enormous proportions, and in Trinity Church the pulpit — with all due deference to the altar — was where the action was. Unlike most Episcopal churches, Trinity was known as a "preaching" church, although it had not been so identified until Phillips Brooks made it so.

What could have been Brooks' appeal? Many of his contemporaries said that he made sense of religion, which could mean that he was not overly fussy about doctrine or theological niceties, for it was certainly the case that he refused to be caught up in the doctrinal disputes and debates of the day. Phillips Brooks was descended from a long line of New England Congregationalists for whom preaching was as sacramental an act as baptism or Holy Communion, who understood the Protestant principle that people have to be able to understand their faith in their own idiom, vernacular religion. Perhaps his appeal was his ability, amply demonstrated in this collection, to communicate complex matters of importance clearly and simply to ordinary listeners, and perhaps his was the art that concealed art. People like what they understand, and when they found that Brooks could make the Christian faith understandable, even within the liturgically inhibiting confines of Episcopal Prayer Book worship, they heard him gladly.

Perhaps another part of his appeal was that he saw his function as relating the human situation to the biblical, and that each contributed to an understanding of the other.

Brooks consistently practiced biblical preaching, which is to say that he understood that part of his task was to open the treasures of the Scriptures to his people; and it was his pastoral concern for the human condition and its relationship to the eternal truths of the Christian gospel that made him a biblical preacher and not merely an orator on religious themes.

Another part of his appeal as commented upon by his contemporaries was the sense they had that Phillips Brooks was preaching directly, and perhaps only, to them. He was accustomed to large, impersonal congregations and audiences, and yet people would comment that they felt as if the rector was speaking directly to their situation, about which he could not possibly have known very much. Unlike his English contemporary Prime Minister William Ewart Gladstone, whom Queen Victoria accused of addressing her as a "public meeting," Brooks seemingly could always speak to a person heart to heart, deep calling unto deep; and to have such a sense of personal appeal, even of relationship, in an age of increasing social mobility and anonymity was an understandable asset in the public work of preaching.

His appeal was not restricted to the pew-renters of Trinity parish, for Brooks was constantly on the circuit throughout the northeast. Hardly a preparatory school in New England was without his presence in its pulpit at least once in every twelve months, where he was popular among both boys and girls; and at Harvard, where he preached regularly and served on the University's Board of Preachers, in the compulsory services of the day he was annually voted the most popular preacher of the year. A measure of Brooks's popularity at Harvard was President Charles William Eliot's invitation to him to become the official Preacher to the University, which Brooks declined on the grounds that he was better suited to parish than to university life. Ordinary people in parish churches, and men of affairs — the "establishment," as it were — in equal measure took to Brooks and regarded him as one of their own; and no preacher in New England, probably since Cotton Mather, dominated the cultural landscape more than did Phillips Brooks.

Something of his appeal can be found in these sermons, which obviously spoke to Ellen Wilbur from practically archival dust, for not even their poor physical state could inhibit the power of the language and ideas of Phillips Brooks. Even in print, and at the remove of a century, Brooks sounds well, which is no small thing when few sermons last beyond lunchtime.

Phillips Brooks has survived the celebrity of his age, the obscurity of the twentieth century, now to speak with new and convincing power to the twenty-first century in a voice as fresh as ever it was. In the first Lyman Beecher Lectures on Preaching at Yale University, founded by the famous preacher's family to honor the art and discipline of preaching, Phillips Brooks, then at the high noon of his own fame, famously defined preaching as "Truth through Personality" in a definition that has achieved iconic status in homiletics. He spoke, of course, of Jesus, the Incarnate Word, but he himself was no small incarnation of the truth of the gospel. By the power of his words and through the medium of his personality Phillips Brooks brought many to the way of life; and thanks to the energy and commitment of Ellen Wilbur he is now able to perform this great work for a new century, and for generations yet to come.

PETER J. GOMES
*Sparks House*
*Cambridge, Massachusetts*
*February 1, 2003*

# *Preface*

Two years ago I began to read Phillips Brooks' sermons. As a member of Trinity Church, where Brooks was rector for more than twenty years, I'd heard what an extraordinary preacher the man was, who'd packed the church on Sundays so that every seat in the enormous room was taken and all the standing room was filled. I knew that Phillips Brooks had come to Trinity not long after the Civil War, and I was curious to see how his sermons would sound more than a century later to a modern ear. I wasn't prepared for the timeless voice that seemed electrically alive and present, the passion with which it spoke, or the power of its teachings. It was a ringing voice that shook my spirit to attention.

I wanted to buy a collection of Brooks' sermons and was disappointed to discover that all his published work was out of print. I found it wasn't easy to gain access to his books. At the Cambridge Public Library out of a ten-volume series of Brooks' sermons only two books remained, and these were damaged relics held together by rubber bands. The same was the case at all the local libraries, where holdings of Brooks' works were uniformly scanty. The few volumes I culled were in such fragile shape that more than once, as I was reading a particularly fine sermon, the pages broke and crumbled in my hands. It was shocking to discover something precious at the moment when it was destroyed.

The sermons that I read stayed with me. Sometimes, while reading them, I felt as if my mind were bathed in light, and at the end was left with a sense of lingering illumination. There was no question that Brooks' words taught and changed me, and if I found his thoughts so luminous and startling, I was sure that others would as well. I asked an acquaintance at Trinity if she would study some of the sermons with me during Lent. In the end there were three of us reading from xeroxed copies one of us had made. When we met one evening to discuss them, it was evident that we were all stirred and equally excited, like people who had come upon a treasure.

My sister-in-law helped me to take out Brooks' books from Harvard's Widener Library. I'd never read a book of sermons in my life, and now wanted to read nothing but Phillips Brooks. There was something wondrous about the loving voice with which he spoke and the utter faith which underlay and glorified all of his preaching. Here was a poet of a speaker, but more than that a man whose loftiness of mind and heart shone through his words in such a way that made it easy to imagine rooms of hushed, uplifted people pinned on him, as much astonished by the man as by his teachings. If you were willing to read through the first demanding pages of Brooks' texts, you reached a place that was sublime where he laid out his lesson and his guiding view, spurring your soul, as though a bridge had been thrown down over a chasm on the road to God.

Reading the sermons often seemed inimical to modern life. I found you couldn't study them with music or voices sounding in the background. To take them in required concentration. Also, a sense of unrushed calm and open listening, like the expectant mood of a church congregation when all eyes are upraised and fixed hard on the rector in his pulpit. Not surprising (though it did amaze me) was the fact that if you read Brooks' sermons to yourself out loud, they often burst to life, as much as if you'd been half-deaf to them before, and now were clearly hearing.

One day, while I was hiking with a friend out in North Andover, I spoke of little else but Brooks, what a wrong it was that his work was not available to a wide readership, how I wished that I could make a new collection of his sermons, but felt this job must be the responsibility of a respected theologian, a bishop, or a religious scholar, not a short story writer and flawed Christian like me. That day I can remember feeling almost haunted by the man. I hadn't yet read any biography of his life and didn't know of his family's connection to North Andover. As we were driving home at dusk, we passed the village green. There before us in the dimming light was the looming statue of a man. My friend, who'd seen the bust of Phillips Brooks at Trinity, was the one who recognized Brooks' features. We stopped the car, and I remember that it was stunning, almost alarming, to see the actuality of this huge figure which matched the presence burning in my mind. That strange, coincidental moment became the impetus for this book.

I went to see Samuel Lloyd, Trinity's rector, with the idea. His enthusiasm was elating, and I asked him if I could present him with a selection of Brooks' sermons for his consideration by the end of summer. In the fall I sent ten sermons to him and gave the same collection to Peter Gomes, rector of The Memorial Church at Harvard University.

Perhaps someone will soon republish all of the two hundred sermons that were once so widely read by people here in America and abroad. In the meantime, it is my hope that this new collection will honor some of Phillips Brooks' finest work, and keep it living in the world.

Readers of this book may be interested to know that "The Withheld Completions of Life" and "The Consolations of God" are two of Brooks' earliest sermons, written at the beginning of his preaching life. Although at times their language sounds more dated than the ageless voice of other sermons, I chose to include them for their passion, beauty, and powerful ideas, which seem, like all of Brooks' best work, to speak directly to the human soul.

ELLEN WILBUR

# The Secret of the Lord

*The secret of the Lord is with them that fear him.*

Psalm xxv.14

E very living thing which is really worth the knowing has a secret in
it which can be known only to a few. The forms and methods of
things lie open to whoever chooses to study them, but the essential
lives of things are hidden away where some special sympathy must find
them. We can all recognize how true this is of men. A certain shrewd
observation of mankind soon lets us into the ordinary laws of human
working. A careful watching of any fellow-man soon lets us understand
his laws, and we can say pretty surely how he will act in any certain circumstances; but behind all such shrewd observations and all that they
discover there is something that every man holds back from us; and the
more of a man he is, the more conscious we are of this reserve. It is this
secret of men that gives them their interest. They are not mere ma-
chines whose mechanism you can completely master. The man is in behind and deeper than his actions. Many a man's actions you comprehend, but only with a very few do you feel that you have really got hold
of the secret of the man. You know the outside of a hundred houses in
town, but only of your own and one or two others do you know the inner chambers.

The more of a man a man is, the more secret is the secret of his life,
and the more plain and frank are its external workings. A small and

I

shallow man tries to throw a mystery about the mere methods of his life, he tries to make his ways of living seem obscure. Where he goes, how he makes his fortune, whom he talks with, what his words mean, who his friends are — he is very mysterious about all these, and all because the secret of his life is really weak, because he is conscious that there is no really strong purpose of living which he himself understands. It is a shallow pool which muddies its surface to make itself look deep. But a greater man will be perfectly frank and unmysterious about these little things. Anybody may know what he does and where he goes. His acts will be transparent, his words will be intelligible. Yet all the while everyone who looks at him will see that there is something behind all, which escapes the closest observation. The very clearness of the surface will show how deep the water is, how far away the bottom lies. There is hardly a better way to tell a great man from a little one.

Whether we can discover such a secret of life in other men or not, everyone is more or less aware of it in himself. We all know how little other people know about us. The common saying that other people know us better than we know ourselves is only very superficially true. They do see certain tricks in us which we are not aware of; they do see the absurdities of some of our behavior which we think is dignified; but, if we are at all thoughtful and self-observant, they do not get at the secret of our life as we know it. They do not know the mainspring, the master-motive as we do who feel it slowly unwinding and moving all the mechanism. It often arms us and puts vigor in us to be sure of this. Our light behavior may be regulated by a reference to men's superior knowledge of it, but no man can live strongly who is not sure that after all he understands himself better than any other man can understand him. His own conscience, his own consciousness he must not despise. He is only a miserable weathercock if he does.

Such is the secrecy of a man's secret. But still there are with all of us some men who possess our secret more or less. The secret of a man's life I have made to consist in its purpose. It is its spirit, its intention. Any man may know what I do, but hardly any man can know as I know myself what I know by doing it. It is the same with every living thing. Nature with her great life has her botanists who tell us what she does with wonderful accuracy, and she has her poets who catch her meaning and her spirit. The institutions of our land show their workings to every keen-eyed politician, but they open their heart, their genius, only to a few philosophic statesmen.

Now with regard to men, we can see something of what is necessary before one can read another's secret. Who is it that can really get at the motive, the genius of your life? What must his qualifications be? It is not mere curiosity — we know how that shuts up the nature which it tries to read. It is not mere awkward good-will; that, too, crushes the flower which it tries to examine. What is it? It must have certain elements in it which we all know. And the first, the most fundamental, the most necessary of them all, is respect. Just think of it. You cannot show the real secret of your life, the spring and power of your living, to any man who does not respect you. Not merely you will not, but you cannot. Is it not so? A man comes with impertinent curiosity and looks into your window, and you shut it in his face indignantly. A friend comes strolling by and gazes in with easy carelessness, not making much of what you may be doing, not thinking it of much importance, and before him you cover up instinctively the work which was serious to you and make believe that you were only playing games. So it is when men try to get hold of the secret of your life. No friendship, no kindliness, can make you show it to them unless they evidently really feel as you feel that it is a serious and sacred thing. There must be something like reverence or awe about the way that they approach you. It is the way in which children shut themselves up before their elders because they know their elders have no such sense as they have of the importance of their childish thoughts and feelings.

Now it is just this respect, this reverence, I take it, that is expressed in my text by the word "fear." You must believe that there is something deep in nature or you will find nothing there. You must have an awe of the mystery and sacredness in your fellow-man, or his mystery and sacredness will escape you. And this sense of mystery and sacredness is what we gather into that word "fear." It is the feeling with which you step across the threshold of a great deserted temple or into some vast dark mysterious cavern. It is not terror. That would make one turn and run away. Terror is a blinding and deafening emotion. Terror shuts up the apprehension. You do not get at the secret of anything which frightens you, but fear, as we use it now, is quite a different emotion. It is a large, deep sense of the majesty and importance of anything, a reverence and respect for it. Without that no man can understand another. And so "The secret of a man is with them that fear him."

And now we pass over to our text. David speaks of the "secret of the Lord." Have we not reached some sort of notion of what he means by that and by what he says of it, that it "is with them that fear him"? God's works are everywhere. The world is full of them, and any man with open and observing eyes may know a great deal about God from all His works. It is not hard to read His power. His wisdom shines upon us from a multitude of adaptations. But all the time we know these are not God. Somewhere behind them all, somewhere within them, moving them all and yet infinitely greater and more spiritual than all of them, there is He, the Maker and the Guider of the whole. He has His inner character. He has His dispositions towards us whom these works of His touch at last. He has His purposes and intentions in them all.

And some souls we can see that seem to have attained to and to live in all this. How clearly it marks the difference between two classes of believers in and servants of God! One knows God's methods and tries to do His will, sees what He wants and catches it up and tries hard to accomplish it, works on from task to task, taking each as it is given but not knowing in the least what it all means, only knowing that God has ordered it. That is one sort of life. We will not dare disparage it. It stirs up our enthusiasm as we gaze upon it. But there is another which we know is better. Another soul does understand what God means by it all, does enter into God's idea. It sees the love which lies behind every commandment and, continually cognizant of the perfect divine nature, it feels at once how far it is from that nature, and knows that the one purpose which God has concerning it is to draw it towards and shape it into Himself. The making of man like Himself by the power of love — that, in one word, is the purpose of God which this soul sees, feels everywhere, enlightening, interpreting everything. That is the secret of the Lord!

My dear friends, do not say that such an idea as that can really make no difference, that one man may have possession of it, and another may not have it, and yet their lives be just alike. Rather think how different your life would be if you had everywhere and always this secret of the Lord. What is your life? Is it this circle of actions that men see? Perhaps it might not alter. Perhaps you might go on rising and sleeping, eating and drinking, and doing business, just as you do now. But if your life really is the way you do these things, the comfort and the culture that you get out of them, the good you do to others and yourself by doing them, would not that all be altered if in every one of them you knew and felt the presence and power of God loving you tenderly, and by His love making you like Himself. The hammer strikes the iron that is on the anvil, and if the iron knows only the power of the hammer it yields doggedly and hardly to the blows. But behind the power is a purpose. In the fine and gentle brain of Him who holds the hammer is a thought of beauty, an untold, unembodied fancy, a secret which He is purposing to work out into expression in this stiff, black iron. Let the iron grow conscious of that purpose, let the secret of the worker be with the material on which he works, and will it make no difference? The enthusiasm of the worker enters into the work. It struggles itself towards its destined shape. Every blow that falls on it is a delight. The rigid vine tries to curl itself in leaves and round itself in fruit. All life has entered into it with the secret of its Lord.

It seems as if, looking back in history, we could see certain ages which evidently had, and certain other ages which had not, the secret of the Lord. There have been times when the general heart of men seemed to be impressed with the spiritual purposes of God, times when the life was more than meat to multitudes of men. The certainty that God meant something spiritual by it all has run through everything; it has inspired the king upon his throne, the general at his army's head, and the women at their work. Blunders enough such times have to show, more blunders than the times which smoothed all the great deeps of purpose out of the world and thought that God had no secret. It is not strange that hard and clumsy hands should make their blunders just in proportion to the fineness of the things they handle. But still these spiritual times, such times as those of the great Reformation, stand out forever in their difference from other ages, touched with a diviner color, and lifting up their heads with a more humble and majestic dignity.

5

We know in our own lives, I am sure, something of such a difference. Some times there have been when God's secret has been with us, when this divine purpose, the making of us into a holiness like His own, has shone out everywhere. It has startled us when we least expected it. It has lurked in our pleasures and our pains; we have unfolded some joy which chance seemed to have dropped in our way, and there it was; we have taken up some burden that lay in our path, and there it was again. We have followed out a friendship, and by and by we have seen how through that friendship God was bringing us to Himself. Again, a friendship has snapped and broken, and in its ruin we have found the same purpose manifest; we and our friend were to go by different roads, but both to go still to the same end, to holiness in God. Sometimes, it may be, such a perception of God's purposes, such a hold on the secret of the Lord, has been with us for a long time; and then perhaps we have lost it; it has seemed incredible that there was any spiritual meaning in life. Mere duties, duties, duties, hard and objectless, waves out of a mysterious ocean of divine authority, which brought no word from the divine character, which said nothing intelligible to us, have beat monotonously on our life. But we could never quite forget the sight that we had seen; we never could deny that there was a purpose though we had lost sight of it, that God had a secret though we had lost it.

Let us not think that this strange, painful alternative comes of God's design. God's secret is not kept secret by any arbitrary cruelty of His. He does not tantalize or taunt us. He shows all of us always all of Himself that He can. That is the basis of all faith about Him. Without believing that first of all, we could believe nothing. And the Incarnation was the opening of every door into this secret of God — this deep abiding spiritual purpose of His nature. Whoever really knows Christ knows God's secret — "that men may be perfect even as He is."

It is strange indeed as we look back to see how men have cheated themselves with strange beliefs about the way in which God, the great Father, gave the knowledge of Himself to His children. "There was a secret of the Lord" — that men understood full well, a close and loving friendship which let man into the deep purposes of God — and some men had this secret and delighted in it, and other men, wishing perhaps that they had it, went through life without it. What made the difference? And it was natural for men to think of favoritism, to get some idea of arbitrary preference, of some election, by which God gave to one choice child what He denied to the rest. There is always this tendency to make that arbitrary which is essential. It seems as if it in some way relieved the burden of thought and responsibility. But any idea of election is really at war with man's primary thought of God, and ultimately makes men sceptics. The only tenable idea is that God will give Himself just as largely and as speedily to man as is possible. Live in that idea as the first certainty of your religion, always, I beg you. And the possibility must depend on man's receptive power. The impossibility, if there is any, must be not in God, but in man. That, too, is sure. Now it is just this receptive power which is described here under the great word, "fear." Apply to God all that we said of man, and we shall know what "fear" means here. It is that large awful sense of God's nature which opens our nature to His coming in. It is not that fear which love "casts out," but a fear which abides with and makes part of and is essential to entire love. Tell me, can you ever love any person perfectly whom you do not also fear, for whom you have not some such reverence as makes you dread to hurt or to offend them, whose anger you are not afraid of? Men call it love sometimes when these are absent, but love without respect has lost the substance and the essence of itself, and is mere passion. Men say, "I cannot love God if I have to fear Him." My dear friend, I always want to say, you cannot love God unless you fear Him, that is the true truth.

There is indeed something Old Testament-like in the specification of fear as the quality to which God can reveal Himself most deeply. But the Old Testament and the New Testament are not in conflict. At the bottom they are really one. They show the brazen and the silver sides of the same truth. And very often now I think we feel the need, both for ourselves and other people, of the Old Testament side of truth. We cannot overestimate the love of God. We cannot say too often to ourselves, "God loves us." But there is something — have we not all felt it as we have read the religious books and listened to a good deal of the preaching that is most in vogue? — there is something of an easy familiarity with God, which loses His secret. The frightened devotee who stands afar off and in mortal terror sends his prayers through a multitude of intermediaries to a God whom he dare not approach, he certainly is not learning deeply of God, the secret of God is not with him. But, on the other hand, the ready zealot, who pours his gushing prayers into the divine ear as he would talk to his own boon companion, neither is he understanding the Almighty. Always there is before us that figure of the publican, who would not lift up so much as his eyes to heaven, who beat upon his breast. There was fear, but there was love certainly, and there was knowledge certainly. One misses very often, in our modern feeling towards God, that exquisite mingling of reverence and familiarity which we see in the apostles' intercourse with Christ. As soon as religion becomes trustful and affectionate, it is apt to grow weakly sentimental and fondly garrulous. The mediaeval nun talking of Christ like a mortal lover, or the modern exhorter singing of Jesus as if He were to be won by fulsome epithets and pathetic tunes — in these we feel the lack of something solid and serene and simple which was in Peter and in John. What was that something? How can we name it except thus, that it was the fear of Jesus? As we read all their life with Him, and see them calmly gathering more and more of Him into themselves, it seems as if those words told the whole story. The secret of their Lord was with them because they feared Him.

Sometimes we can seem to see such a Christianity now. Earnest without excitement, loving without familiarity, a man or a woman is always near to Christ and yet never touches Him, never speaks His name, without awe. None of the first sacredness has melted away with time. The prayer tonight is fuller of the sense of what a stupendous thing it is to pray, than was the first faltering petition. Duty by which the soul expresses itself to God is quiet and not feverish, but full of deep delight and sacredness. Love deepens every hour, but reverence is always deepening with it, and to this ever-deepening reverence and love the nature and purposes of God are always opening; and so in such a life, not far off in the apostolic ages, but walking here among us now, the same truth is fulfilled again, and the "secret of the Lord is with them that fear him."

How, then, can we know God? Men bring their different directions, and we take them all and see some good in almost all of them, but after

8

all we come to this, that the only good in any of them must be in the power they have to bring in us a loving fear of God, to which alone enlightenment can come.

One man says, "If you want to know God, you must be punctilious about religious duty; you must go to church; you must omit no form; you must be where God is; so you shall see Him." Yes, just so far as rite or sacrament does really show you His majesty, just so far as all these things do really make it a more terrible thing to you to do what God disallows, just so far they are rich in revelation. Not in themselves! They are mere windows; keep them pure and hold them Godward and then through them you shall see God.

Another man has quite another thing to say. To know God you must go among His works; His world will tell you of Him. Not in the church but in the woods; not out of the Bible but out of the sky you will read what He is. Again, remember, if that be the religion to which you are most drawn, that no flush of delight in nature, no exultation in the opening spring or sober seriousness of autumn days, does really bring God's secret to you unless it really gives you a personal fear of Him, a dread of wronging Him, a jealous, loving watchfulness over yourself for His sake.

I know that Christ Himself had this. The fear of God, a fear that is sublimely compatible with love — we talk of it, we try to picture what it is, but look at Him and see it perfectly. Was not He always fearing God? Was there a dread in all His life like the dread of doing what God would not wish? And yet what love! Into that loving fear flowed the whole secret of the Lord, that knowledge of the Father that made the Son's perfect unity with Him.

Both in the temple and in the world of nature Jesus gathered this fear and all the knowledge that it brought. From both of them we may gather it too, but most of all, above both these, we are to gather it from Him. There is the final answer to one question which I most wish to leave with you. How shall I have God's secret? By fearing Him! How shall I fear Him? By most clearly seeing Him! How shall I see Him? Here, where He is manifest in Christ. Really know Him. Get truly face to face with that Person. By true obedience understand what He is, and then the fearfulness of God, the greatness of His nature and His love will take possession of you, and in that atmosphere the secret of the Lord shall come to you and be with you. Can you understand that? Is there anything in your experience already to interpret it? Have you indeed found that, as you knew Christ more, God was more full of majesty and more near to you both at once? Then keep on! Heaven at last will be the perfect sight of Christ. To them that see Him perfectly the fear of God will come, a fear full of love and glory; and then through the fear will come the knowledge, and the secret of the Lord shall be with those that fear Him more and more perfectly forever.

# The First Sunday in Advent

—ɱ—

*Till we all come in the unity of the faith, and of the knowledge of the Son of God, unto a perfect man, unto the measure of the stature of the fullness of Christ.*

Ephesians iv.13

If any entire stranger were to come today into our service and watch it as it moves along from step to step, one thing would become evident to him in it all. He would see that we were *beginning something.* Everything, apparently, is starting fresh. And if he looked along the services of the other Sundays that are to follow this he would see that it is a whole long year that we are commencing. A course that runs on through the next twelve months opens today. On through the deepening winter, on through the opening spring, on into the far-off warmth of next summer, until another autumn closes on us, is to run the course of services beginning on this Advent Sunday. It is the Church's New Year's Day. And one thing more would strike him if he were observant. He would see that all this year is filled and shaped by the life of a *Person.* One man's biography sweeps through it all, and every season is colored with the aspect in which it finds the great pervading life of Jesus Christ. Men's fortunes and employments will change as they always do. Success and failure, health and sickness, life and death, will come with all the changing months around to next December; but through them all, as if it were something that lay deeper than their changes, as if it were the presence in which and even the power by which all men failed or succeeded, lived or died, will run the story of Him who was born in Bethlehem and ascended into heaven from the Mount of Olives. And the observant stranger who saw this would have thus found the central truth of Christianity. He would have seen represented that presence and power which all Christian life, whether of church or soul, is always trying to realize — the presence and power of the Incarnation; the truth that all of human life is lived in the presence of, is represented by, and may be filled with and inspired by the life of the great Son of Man, who in a hundred senses *lived for* all men; in whose experiences all human experiences ought to find their key and their solution; who became completely what we are that we might come in everything to be like Him.

Christ was both the Redeemer and the Type of human life, the Savior and the Pattern of men at once. We too much separate His two great offices, which really are not distinguishable. He could not have been our Savior without being our Pattern; and even in the most mysterious functions of this Saviorhood there is always something in which we can pattern ourselves by Him. It follows, then, that all this life whose story we begin today is not merely a remote inimitable transaction wrought for every man's salvation, but is also the type of every man's existence. It is the great representative existence. All that happened to Christ's humanity belongs to the perfect ideal picture of every human life. As we stand, then, upon the height of Advent Sunday and look along the stages of the life of Jesus which the Church will one by one commemorate, we are really looking along the history of universal human life, and so the possible, the perfect life of every man. Each stage was perfect in its development in Him, but each stage, however imperfectly lived, belongs to all men. The Christian year becomes, then, in one very true view of it, the picture of a human life from its first suggested promise to its latest effective influence upon the earth. Let me lead you to this thought and its developments. Let us see how each season of the Church's year presents a true period in and experience of every truly human life, represented by and worked out in the pattern of the human life of Jesus. I hope that such a study may do something to bring the perfect divine and human life of Christ closer to these lives of ours; for that is what all our worship and preaching are for; that is the greatest happiness and blessing that can come to any man.

The Church's year begins with Christ's advent; then comes His epiphany, then His suffering and death, and then the giving of His Spirit. Through all of these we shall pass in these next few months.

1. Take first the *advent.* It was not suddenly and unannounced that Jesus came into the world. He came into a world that had been prepared for Him. The whole Old Testament is the story of a special preparation. The key to Jewish history is the anticipation of His coming. And we have not begun to understand the vastness of His mission unless we know that not merely the education of Judea, but the education of the whole world, was and is aimed at the preparation for the time when Jesus Christ should come to be its Master. You go into some heathen island now and preach Christ, and every readiness of nature to appreciate and take Him, which has been wrought out by all their religious struggles, is but another sign and illustration of how God prepares the advent of His Son. And then inside of the Judean history we have the special preparation — the story which we read this morning, the mission and ministry of John the Baptist. Only when all was ready, only in the fullness of His time, did Jesus come.

And now what shall we say about the lives of other men — the men of whom He was the representative and the chief? Have they their advents too? It is easy to believe it about the greatest of them. It is easy to think that those who have gathered the richness of the world into themselves and turned its currents of action or thought — easy to think of Moses, Charlemagne, Luther, Bacon, Shakespeare — that God prepared the world against their coming and sent them when the world was ready. The ages seem to make their advents. But it is hard to think the same of common people such as you and I. It seems as if our lives might have been dropped anywhere — three thousand years ago as well as now, and on the banks of the Nile as well as on the shores of Massachusetts Bay. Hard as it is, great as the strain which it puts on all our low habits of thinking about ourselves, the Bible is a strong and glorious call to men to gird up the loins of their minds and believe that God had a place for them and put them in their own place. It has these two truths, which it insists upon everywhere: that God cares separately for every man, and that every man has his own individual personal character. Personal divine care and personal human character — these two ideas are bright in all the Bible; in both the Testaments, in David and in Paul alike. Take those two truths together and they would blend in the conviction that God surely could not send His souls at random into the world, but for each a place must be hollowed in the plain of time and filled with all that could bring that soul to its best completeness. And this conviction, gathered out of the Bible's whole treatment of humanity, is set forth with representative clearness in the story of the advent of the Son of Man.

This, then, is the beginning of a life. It goes back before the moment when the man is here, a visible fact upon the earth. It lays hold of the thought of God which runs back into eternity. God knew your nature. He had a plan and pattern of your being in His mind. As David says, His eyes did see your substance, yet being imperfect, and in His book were all your members written. Knowing you, He made ready a place for you, He shaped a cradle for you in the ages, and when it was all done He laid your new life in it — the advent before the nativity.

What influence shall it have upon a man for him to know all this about his life — to know that it was contemplated and the world made ready for it before he was born? Shall it not give him, first, *a deep reverence for his own life?* Shall it not shake him free from that moral laziness which cloaks itself in the disguise of modesty, and make him accept the responsibilities and duties of a being for whom God has made the earth and the ages ready?

And shall it not make him *docile,* teaching him to look not to his own self-will, but to the God who chose his place for him, to know what, living in just that place, he ought to be? Responsibility and docility — these qualities of which the life of Jesus was so full — must fill the life of every man who believes in his own advent.

2. After the advent comes the *nativity.* The promised Christ is born. We can see what that meant in the history of Jesus. No longer prophesied and anticipated, at last the great typal life was a real fact in the world — a visible fact with all its possibilities contained within it. It was, indeed, but a poor helpless child at Bethlehem, but in its being there was really wrapped up all that that child was to grow to and to be

and do. No wonder that Christmas Day has been so sacred to all those who believed in Jesus Christ; for it has seemed to sum up in itself every association and meaning of His life. *Birth,* the second fact in existence, the actual appearing of a being planned in the thought of God, had first in Christ this deep and comprehensive value, but it has kept that same value always.

Carry it over now to other men. Why is it that we celebrate the birthdays of great men? Is it not because all that they were and did seems to be gathered up into that critical moment when their life first was present as a true, real fact among the lives of men? And remember, here, just as before, our distinctions between great men and common men are mostly arbitrary and accidental. We are all so little and all so great in God's sight. So that the birth of *any* man, the beginning of *any* new life, is a great and solemn thing. How hard it is sometimes to make it seem so to ourselves! With all this swarm of men about us, how in our lower moments we wonder, after all, whether it is more than the buzzing of a little wiser bees about their hive, or the clustering of a little bigger ants around their ant-hill! What matter whether there be one more or less? What matter whether one be taken away or one added to the uncounted number? What matter death or birth? That is the low way of looking at it all. The higher way, catching the spirit of the Lord's nativity, when the angels sang in heaven because a Man was born, and the very stars were conscious of His coming, sees the true dignity, the almost awful solemnity of a human birth. It wonders whether there is anything in the universe more critical and sacred than for a new human life to begin here on the earth. These other worlds about us may have the same mysterious, infinite event. In them, too, spiritual beings — beings with characters like men and women — may be born, and then there is in them the same solemnity that there is here. But if not — if they have no life of character, nothing corresponding to our personality — then no splendor or exquisiteness of physical life that they may have to boast can make them for a moment rivals in dignity and interest of this little planet that swims in their midst. For here men are born. Each from the moment of his birth has his own singleness and unity. Each may be saved or lost. Each may do right or wrong. Each may be like God or like Satan. Each has a capacity of happiness or misery as yet unfathomed. Each may become glorious or horrible — glorious with a spiritual luster that no physical brilliance of any brightest star can compare with, or horrible with a tragical destruction that no burned and blasted planet can begin to match. All this is wrapped up in every man's birth, his whole power of separate existence; and so every man who really knows the sacredness of his own birth, who has learned from the wonders that surrounded the entrance of God into our flesh what a wonderful thing it is for any man to begin to live in the life which the Incarnation illuminated, must go through life strong and alert, with a clear sense of his own personality, never losing himself in the mass and crowd, keeping his independence, thinking his own thoughts, and feeling his own feelings — *being a man,* as he never loses sight of his birth, the time when he *began* to be a man.

3. After Advent and Christmas in the Church's year comes the *Epiphany,* which celebrates the manifestation of Christ to those entirely outside of His own life and all its first associations. The world made ready for Him and His birth complete, now He must show His influence upon the world. The purpose of His coming must be seen, that men may be something different because He is here; may be drawn away from themselves to Him. I want you to see how this new stage in Christ's life represents the next stage in the fullest and highest life of man; for it is most important, and it is so easily forgotten and neglected. A man's place is made ready for him in the mind of God; the man's life is set here as a positive, clear fact; and what comes next? There is no doubt what ought to come. That life must *tell.* It must go out beyond itself. It must have *influence.* It must testify and supplement the mere fact of its existence by making other existences be something which they would not be without it. This seems so plain. This is so clearly set forth in the great typical life of Jesus. Can you conceive of an incarnation in which it should not have been prominent? Can you picture to yourself God coming into this world and then living a perfectly self-contained life — one that recognized no relations with and exercised no power over other lives about Him? No! The epiphany followed immediately on the advent, and the nativity. Not by an effort; it was the next natural and necessary stage. It was a true epiphany. He merely showed Himself. He let His life go forth on other lives. He let His great

light shine before men. But how many there are who realize their advent and their nativity who have never conceived for themselves of an epiphany! There are so many men who believe in their own place in the world, and are conscious of their own personal nature with its capacities and needs, who never have gone any further — never have dreamed that they were put here *where* they are, and made to be *what* they are, in order that other men might be something else through them. This is one of the heresies of life which men are not ashamed to own. They put it into philosophic shapes. There are theories of self-culture which are printed in books, taught in our schools, given as very gospels to our children as they grow up, which would be just exactly the same that they are now if no such dream as a possible duty of usefulness and influence from that child to other people had ever entered into the thought of God or man.

Hear what a child is taught. Is not this mostly what is said to him? "You are born into this rich and gorgeous nineteenth century. You are the 'heir of all the ages.' All the thought, discovery, invention, progress of the centuries have been fitting this world for your coming. And now, when the world is all ready, here you are." That is the lesson of his *advent*. And then he is told: "*You* are born into this world; *you*, a separate, distinct, new being; *you*, with a personal life; *you* who are and can be something that no other being in the world can be." That is the lesson of his *nativity*. He takes them both, and the result of both as they sink into his soul is a conviction and a resolution full of selfishness: "I will study, I will work and think, I will claim my place here — all that I may be myself completely, that I may cultivate myself." It rings through all our books and colleges, through all our homes and stores, this gospel of self-culture. "Be strong, be rich, be wise, be good." What for? "Why, so that you may be wise and rich and strong and good." The endless circle with its bright monotonous round. No wonder that so many young men are asking in the bottom of their hearts questions of most terrible skepticism: "What is the use? Is it worthwhile to be wise and strong and rich and good?" Ah, you must find the use *outside yourself*. You must let your light shine *before men*, that they may see your good works, and glorify your Father which is in heaven. You must complete your advent and nativity with an epiphany of yourself. Then it will seem well worthwhile to light your human light most brilliantly and keep it trimmed most vigilantly. Do you ask me how? Do you not see that it is impossible for anyone to tell you? The sun or the street lamp might as well ask *how* to light the passenger. Only shine *toward* your brethren's lives, only be your best in their direction. It must be a true epiphany, a real showing of yourself to other men. As different and characteristic as yourself is will be the light you give them. Perhaps you will illustrate for them some truth, perhaps you will inspire them with some hope, perhaps you will teach them how to do their work. The methods will decree themselves if only you, like Christ, are what you are, not for yourself, but for your fellow-men; if only, like Him, you have not only an advent and a nativity, but an epiphany. Put these two texts together, for they belong together; the same Christ spoke them: "The Son of Man came not to be ministered unto, but to minister, and give his life a ransom for many"; and "As Thou hast sent Me into the world, even so have I also sent them into the world."

4. But we must pass on. After the Advent, the Nativity, and the Epiphany in the Church's year comes *Lent,* with its preparation for and culmination in *Good Friday,* opening suddenly into the glorious light of *Easter Day.* What does this mean? The life of Jesus, prepared for before His birth, introduced into the world at Bethlehem, then brought into contact with and influence upon the lives of men, finally completes itself in suffering. Remember we are speaking now about Christ's life and death, not with reference to the mysterious redemptive efficacy that was in it, but as the great human life, the representative life that set forth the ideal experience and culture of a human soul. And surely it does not fail us here. Whatever else comes to a life, there is a final grace and greatness which it cannot have until it has been touched by pain. I do not speak it sentimentally. I do not mean the mere pathetic romance which gives a charm to the story of the unfortunate. I mean the very stuff and qualities of our manhood — those things which make us really and completely men. They are not brought out in their manliest vigor until we have suffered. Often the suffering is of a kind men do not see. Physical pain, the sickness which makes one tremble as he walks, and takes the color from the cheek, is the most evident, but it is the smallest kind of suffering. But whenever you have seen a man

leaving his crudity and childishness behind him and really growing mature, however men may say carelessly, "Oh, *he* has never known what it is to suffer," you may know better. That maturity of character is as sure a sign of some healthy experience of pain, however secret, as the brilliancy and clearness of a bit of glass is of the fire through which it has passed. The qualities which nothing but hard contact with suffering can make are not mere pleasing graces; they are the completing qualities of manhood, the very stuff and fiber of a man — self-knowledge, humility, patience, sympathy, and a constant consciousness of God. Can you have a complete man without these, and can you have these unless in some way the man has suffered? This is the reason why it is so universal. You think you know exceptions. But, my dear friend, what do you know about it? The men you call exceptions perhaps have been the very deepest in the sea of pain. You are pouring out your sympathy on some complaining grumbler who has lost a little money, and thinking how painless is the life of a brave man who refuses to grumble, but whose dearest hopes have been broken into fragments, and the ideals which were his very life all disappointed. You do not wrong him by denying him your petty sympathy, but you do wrong yourself in making too much of the little trouble and failing to see with what a great manly education of sorrow God is training *all* His children.

"It became Him, for whom are all things, and by whom are all things, in bringing many sons unto glory, to make the Captain of their salvation perfect through sufferings." When the vase is all shaped into its strong, beautiful form, when the artist's hand has lavished its best skill upon it, then it is quietly laid into the hot oven. By and by it comes out with its lines firm and bright, its surface clear and brilliant, its colors fixed forever. There is a glory after the pain, an Easter after the Lent; but no glory *without* the pain, no Easter without the Lent of character. And who are we that we should grow angry or miserable when we see that great universal treatment by which alone the Son of Man was made perfect, by which alone any son of man ever can be made perfect, drawing near to us or to anyone we love among our fellow-men?

5. After the Lent and Easter comes one stage more — that which is represented by *Whitsunday,* the day of the giving of the Holy Spirit. You remember what Jesus said about the Holy Ghost: "He shall take of

Mine, and shall show it unto you." It was to be the perpetuated work of Christ. After the suffering and death were over, and He was seen no more upon the earth, then His power was really to have but just begun. It should go out and touch men wider and deeper than He had ever done when He was present on the earth. The epiphany was the influence of the visible Christ; the Whitsunday is the influence of the invisible, ascended Christ. Would you call any man's life a great life, even a true life, whose influence stopped the moment his personal, seen presence was removed? It seems to me as if there were hardly any surer test of the reality or unreality, the depth or superficialness of human power. One man seems strong. Here in our community it appears as if he were deciding what men should do or be, which way events should turn. Some day we read in the papers that that man is dead, and from that moment on his power is all gone. It is as if he had never lived. It is as if some hand had with a single touch shifted the machinery so that not the smallest or most insignificant wheel thereafter owned his influence. "None so poor to do him reverence." Another man dies, and it is as if death were the revelation of his force and the beginning of his influence. Men did not know how they loved him till he was taken away. Men did not see the stores of motive and impulse that were in his character till the shell of circumstances was broken through. In his own circle, in the city where he lives, it seems as if he were more powerful when he is seen no more upon the streets than when men met him every day. There has been, as it were, a descent of his spirit, a Pentecost of his departed presence. Oh, there are households among you where some son or daughter who is dead is stronger in the shaping of the daily life than any of the men and women who are still alive. His character is at once a standard and an inspiration. You do what would please him more scrupulously than when he was alive. He conquers your sluggishness and corrects your wilfulness and refines your coarseness every day. To say that he is not *with you* is to make companionship altogether a physical, not at all a spiritual thing. To say that he is absent from you, and that the neighbor of whom you know nothing, for whom you care nothing, and who cares nothing for you, is present with you, is to confuse all thoughts of neighborhood, to put the false for the true, the superficial for the deep.

20

This is the difference of men — those whose power stops with their death, and those whose power really opens into its true richness when they die. The first sort of men have mechanical power. The second sort of men have spiritual power. And the final test and witness of spiritual force is seen in the ability to cast the bodily life away and yet continue to give help and courage and wisdom to those who see us no longer; to be, like Christ, the helper of men's souls even from beyond the grave.

I must stop here. After Whitsunday in the Church's year there come certain Sundays not nominally but really connected with the life of Christ — Trinity Sunday and those that follow it. They represent, I think, the way in which a great life opens into all the various lessons of absolute truth and fills with its influence every field of duty, till it is absolutely world-wide in its range.

THUS I have traced along the Christian year the history that runs through it. It sets up the great human life. The building of the perfect man is the noblest work that can go on in the world. The seasons come and go, the harvests ripen and are gathered in, the mountains are built up and decay; but all these are sights that cannot match in dignity and interest the spectacle of a full, strong man's life. First God prepares for him the place where he is to live. Then his life comes and takes its place, a strong and settled fact. Then it puts forth its power and influences other men. Then suffering comes to it and matures it, but finally it issues out of suffering, refined and triumphant. And at last, when it has passed away out of the world into new regions of activity and growth, it leaves its power behind it to bless men after it is dead. There is nothing so round and perfect as such a life in all the world. It is the very crown of God's creation.

Such a complete life is pictured in the Church's year. It has its Advent, Nativity, Epiphany, Lent, Easter, Whitsunday, Trinity Sunday. It fills the year with its increasing, slowly maturing beauty. This is the true meaning of the year, with all its sacred seasons. Let us be true Churchmen and give it all its richness. Only, dear friends, we do not really honor the venerable beauty of the Church's calendar when we make it a badge of our denominational distinction, or deck its seasons out with all the trickery of colored altar-cloths, purple and white and green, but when we see in it the story of a human life slowly ripened from God's first purpose to the full-grown, glorified manhood standing before God's presence and sending forth God's power to its fellow-men.

We do not dishonor the humanity of Jesus when we thus make it the type of what ours may be. He wanted and He loves to have us use it so. "As I am, so are ye in this world," He declared. Only remember He is not only pattern, but power. We must be like Him, but we cannot be, save as He makes us. We must come to Him, but we can only come to Him by His grace and help.

Standing at the beginning of the Christian year, remembering how He came to redeem us all unto Himself, let us pray for ourselves and one another that the perfect manhood which we see stretching down that year may be complete in each of us; that we may be led as our Lord was led through every stage of growth, till we too enter into the glory of God and leave the spirit of our life behind us to be a live blessing to our brethren when we are what they call dead. This be our Advent prayer.

# The Egyptians Dead upon the Seashore

*And Israel saw the Egyptians dead upon the seashore.*

Exodus xiv.30

It was the Red Sea which the children of Israel had crossed dry-shod, "which the Egyptians essaying to do were drowned." The parted waves had swept back upon the host of the pursuers. The tumult and terror, which had rent the air, had sunk into silence, and all that the escaped people saw was here and there a poor drowned body beaten up upon the bank, where they stood with the great flood between them and the land of their long captivity and oppression. It meant everything to the Israelites. It was not only a wonderful deliverance for them, but a terrible calamity for their enemies. It was the end of a frightful period in their history. These were the men under whose arrogant lordship they had chafed and wrestled. These hands had beaten them. These eyes they had seen burning with scorn and hate. A thousand desperate rebellions, which had not set them free, must have come up in their minds. Sometimes they had been successful for a moment; sometimes they had disabled or disarmed their tyrants; but always the old tyranny had closed back upon them more pitilessly than before. But now all that was over; whatever else they might have to meet, the Egyptian captivity was at an end. Each dead Egyptian face on which they looked was token and witness to them that the power of their masters over them had perished. They stood and gazed at the hard features, set and stern, but powerless in death, and then turned their faces to the desert, and to whatever new unknown experiences God might have in store for them.

It is a picture, I think, of the way in which experiences in this world become finished, and men pass on to other experiences which lie beyond. In some moods it seems to us as if nothing finally got done. When we are in the thick of an experience we find it hard to believe or to imagine that the time will ever come, when that experience shall be wholly a thing of the past and we shall have gone out beyond it into other fields. When we open our eyes morning after morning and find the old struggle on which we closed our eyes last night awaiting us; when we open our door each day only to find our old enemy upon the doorstep; when all our habits and thoughts and associations have become entwined and colored with some tyrannical necessity, which, however it may change the form of its tyranny, will never let us go — it grows so hard as almost to appear impossible for us to anticipate that that dominion ever is to disappear, that we shall ever shake free our wings and leave behind the earth to which we have been chained so long. On the long sea-voyage the green earth becomes inconceivable. To the traveller in the mountains or the desert it becomes very difficult to believe that he shall some day reach the beach and sail upon the sea. But the day comes, nevertheless. Some morning we go out to meet the old struggle, and it is not there. Some day we listen for the old voice of our old tyrant, and the air is still. At last the day does come when our Egyptian, our old master, who has held our life in his hard hands, lies dead upon the seashore, and looking into his cold face we know that our life with him is over, and turn our eyes and our feet eastward to a journey in which he shall have no part. Things do get done, and when they do, when anything is really finished, then come serious and thoughtful moments in which we ask ourselves whether we have let that which we shall know no longer do for us all that it had the power to do, whether we are carrying out of the finished experience that which it has all along been trying to give to our characters and souls.

For while we leave everything behind in time, it is no less true that nothing is wholly left behind. All that we ever have been or done is with us in some power and consequence of it until the end. Is it not most

significant that these children of Israel, whom we behold today looking the dead Egyptians in the face and then turning their backs on
Egypt, are known and appealed to ever afterwards as the people whom
the Lord their God had brought "out of the land of Egypt, out of the
house of bondage"? In every most critical and sacred moment of their
history they are bidden to recall their old captivity. When God most
wants them to know Him, it is as the God of their deliverance that He
declares Himself. The unity of life is never lost. There must not be any
waste. How great and gracious is the economy of life which it involves!
Neither to dwell in any experience always, nor to count any experience
as if it had not been, but to leave the forms of our experiences behind,
and to go forth from them clothed in their spiritual power, which is infinitely free and capable of new activities — this is what God is always
teaching us is possible, and tempting us to do. To him who does it
come the two great blessings of a growing life — faithfulness and liberty: faithfulness in each moment's task, and liberty to enter through
the gates beyond which lies the larger future. "Well done, good servant:
thou hast been faithful over a few things. Enter thou into the joy of thy
Lord."

All this is true, but it is very general. What I want to do this morning is to ask you to think about the special experience to which our text
refers, and consider how one truth is true of that, and of what corre-
sponds to it in all men's lives. It was the end of a struggle which had
seemed interminable. The hostility of Hebrew and Egyptian had gone
on for generations. However their enmity may be disguised or hidden,
the tyrant and the slave are always foes. If hope had ever lived, it had
died long ago. Patient endurance, grim submission, with desperate re-
volt whenever the tyranny grew most tyrannical — these had seemed to
be the only virtues left to the poor serfs. Not to be demoralized and ruined by their servitude, to keep their self-respect, to be sure still that
they were Abraham's children and that Abraham's God still cared for
them, patience and fortitude — these must have been the exhortations
which they addressed to their poor souls as they toiled on in the
brickyard or by the river.

It does not prove anything, if you please, about our present life, but
it certainly sets us to asking new questions about it, perhaps to believ-

ing greater things concerning it, when in our typical story we behold all this changed. Behold, the day came when the chains were broken and the slaves went free. Are, then, our slaveries as hopeless as they seem? Are we condemned only to struggle with our enemies in desperate fight, and shall we not hope to see them some day dead like the Egyptians on the seashore?

Surely it is good for us to ask that question, for nothing is more remarkable than the way in which, both in public and personal life, men accept the permanence of conditions which are certainly some day to disappear. The whole of history which teaches us that mankind does conquer its enemies and see its tyrants by and by lying dead on the seashore, often appears to have no influence with the minds of men, all absorbed as they are in what seems a hopeless struggle. But look around! Where are the Egyptians which used to hold the human body and the human soul in slavery? Have you ever counted? The divine right of rulers, the dominion of the priesthood over the intellect and conscience, the ownership of man by man, the accepted inequality of human lots, the complacent acquiescence in false social states, the use of torture to extort the needed lie, the praise of ignorance as the safeguard of order, the irresponsible possession of power without corresponding duty, the pure content in selfishness — do you realize, in the midst of the cynical and despairing talk by which we are surrounded, can you realize, how these bad tyrants of the human race have lost their power over large regions of human life? They are dead Egyptians. Abominable social theories which fifty years ago, in the old days of slavery, in the old days of accepted pauperism, men stated as melancholy, but hopeless, truisms are now the discarded rubbish of antiquity, kept as they keep the racks and thumb-screws in old castle-dungeons for a tourists' show.

Is there anything more wonderful than the way in which men today are daring to think of the abolition and disappearance of those things which they used to think were as truly a part of human life as the human body, or the ground on which it walks? Ah! my friends, you only show how you are living in the past, not in the present, when you see nothing but material for sport in the beliefs of ardent men and brave societies which set before themselves and humankind the abolition of poverty, the abolition of war, the abolition of ignorance, the abolition of disease, the sweeping away of mere money competition as the motive power of life, the dethronement of fear from the high place which it has held among, aye, almost above, all the ruling and shaping powers of the destiny of man. I recognize in many a frantic cry the great growing conviction of mankind that nothing which ought not to be need be. I hear in many hoarse, ungracious tones man's utterance of his conviction that much which his fathers thought was meant to cultivate their patience by submission, is meant also to cultivate their courage by resistance till it dies. "The Egyptian must die." That is the assurance which is possessing the heart of man.

When any evil does finally perish, then there is something infinitely pathetic in the remembrance of the way in which mankind for generations accepted it as inevitable and drew out of its submission to it such blessing and education as pure submission to the inevitable is able to bestow. The poor man, who thinks his poverty, and the ignorance and servitude which his poverty entails, all right, comforts himself by saying that God made him poor in order that he might be patient and learn to possess his soul in self-respect. By and by when the iniquity of the system under which he has lived gives way and he finds himself admitted to the full rights and duties of a man — what then? Infinitely pathetic, as it seems to me, is the recognition that he wins of the great love and wisdom with which God would not let even that darkness be entirely fruitless of light; but while He was making ready for the fuller life of which the poor man never dreamed, at the same time fed him in the wilderness with manna which the wilderness alone could give, so that no delight of freedom to which he afterwards should come need make him wholly curse or utterly despise the regions of darkness and restraint through which he came to reach it.

Is it not thus that we may always explain at least a part, the best part, of that strange longing with which the world, when it has entered into any higher life, still finds itself looking back to the lower life out of which it has passed? It is not properly regret. It is not a desire to turn back into the darkness. The age of real faith does not covet again the chains of superstition. The world at peace does not ask to be shaken once more by the earthquakes of war. But faith does feel the beauty of

27

complete surrender which superstition kept for its sole spiritual virtue; and peace, with its diffused responsibility, is kindled at the thought of heroic and unquestioning obedience which the education of war produced. Still let superstition and war lie dead. We will not call them back to life; but we will borrow their jewels of silver and jewels of gold as we go forth into the wilderness to worship our God with larger worship. Do you not feel this in all the best progress? Do you not see it in the eyes of mankind, in the depths of the eyes of mankind always, as it turns away from the dead forms of its old masters and goes forth into the years to be; the hoarded power of the past glowing beneath the satisfaction of the present and the fiery hope of the unknown future?

Ah, well, there is always something fascinating in thus dwelling on the fortunes of the world at large, peering, like fortune-telling gypsies, into the open palm which she holds out to all of us. It is fascinating, and is not without its profit. But just as, I suppose, the shrewdest gypsy may often be the most recklessly foolish in the government of her own life, so it is good for us always to turn speedily and ask how the principles which we have been wisely applying to the world, apply to that bit of the world which we are set to live.

Do we believe — you and I — in the death of our Egyptians? What is your Egyptian? Some passion of the flesh or of the mind? — for the mind has its tyrannical passions as well as the flesh. Years, years ago, you became its captive. Perhaps you cannot at all remember when. Perhaps, like these children of Israel, you were born into its captivity. It was your father, or your father's fathers, that first became its slaves. When you first came to know yourself, its chains were on your limbs. As you grew older you knew that it was slavery, but it was such a part of all you were and all you did that you accepted it. That has not made you cease to struggle with it, but it has made you accept struggle hopelessly, as something never to be outgrown and left behind. You have looked forward into the stretch of years, and in prophetic imagination you have seen yourself an old man, still wrestling with the tyranny of your covetousness, or your licentiousness, or your prejudice, getting it down, planting your foot upon its neck, even compelling it to render you, out of the unceasing struggle, new supplies of character; absolutely fixed and determined never to give up the fight until you die — to die fighting. All this is perfectly familiar. Countless noble and patient souls live in such self-knowledge and consecration. But there comes something vastly beyond all these, when the soul dares to believe that its enemy may die, that the lust, or the prejudice, or the covetousness may absolutely pass out of existence, and the nature be absolutely free — sure no doubt to meet other enemies and to struggle till the end, but done with that enemy forever, with that Egyptian finally dead upon the seashore.

When that conviction takes possession of a man, his fight is a new thing. The courage not of desperation, but of certain hope, fills every limb and gives its force to every blow. The victory which the soul believes is coming is here already as a power for its own attainment.

Has a man a right to any such hope as that, or is it the mere dream of an optimistic sermon? I dare appeal to you and ask you whether, in your own experience, God has not sometimes given you the right to such a hope? Are there no foes of your youth which you have conquered and left dead, passing on to greater battles? I am not speaking of the vices which you have miserably left behind, merely because the taste is exhausted and the strength has failed — vices which you would take up again if you were once more twenty years old. Those are poor victories. Those are no victories at all. But I mean this: Whether you are a better or a worse man now than you were twenty years ago. Are there not at least some temptations to which you yielded then to which you know that you can never yield again? Are there not some meannesses which you once thought glorious which now you know are mean? Are there no places where you once stumbled where now you know you can walk firm? I pity you if there are not. Other enemies which you then never dreamed of you have since encountered, but those enemies are done with. The Moabites and Midianites are before you and around you, but the Egyptians are dead. And in their death your right and duty are to read the prophecy of the death of every power which stands up between you and the Promised Land! The appeal is not only to experience. It is to the first Christian truth concerning man. I have preached it to you a thousand times. I will preach it again and again until the end. The great truth of Christianity, the great truth of Christ, is that sin is unnatural and has no business in a human life. The birth of Christ proclaimed that in one tone. His cross proclaimed it in another! And that which is unnatural is not by any necessity permanent. The struggle of all nature is against the unnatural — to dislodge it and cast it out. That beautiful struggle pervades the world. It is going on in every clod of earth, in every tree, in every star, and in the soul of man. First to declare and then to strengthen that struggle in the soul of man was the work of Christ. That work still lingers and fails of full completion, but its power is present in the world. When He takes possession of a nature He quickens that struggle into life. No longer can that nature think itself doomed to evil. Intensely sensitive to feel the presence of evil as he never felt it before, the Christian man instantly and intensely knows that evil is a stranger and an intruder in his life. The wonder is not that it should some day be cast out: the wonder is that it should ever have come in. The victory promised in the sinless Son of man is already potentially attained in the intense conception of its naturalness. This is Christianity.

Is not this the change which you can see coming in the faces of the sinners who meet Jesus and feel His power in the wonderful stories which fill the pages of the Gospels? The first thing which comes to them, the great thing which comes to them all, is a change in their whole conception of life. What used to seem natural comes to seem most unnatural. That which they called unnatural becomes so natural that they cannot see why it should not immediately come to pass. The rich young man's money begins to fade in his hand, and he feels its tyranny passing away. The Magdalen's face grows luminous with a new vision of purity as the only true human life. Bigotry looks to Nicodemus what it really is. The simple naturalness in the hope that the children of God should live the life of God comes and folds itself around each of them. And in that atmosphere of their new life the old life with its old bondages dies.

You see how positive all this is. And that, too, seems to me to be depicted in the old Hebrew story, which we are using for our parable. It was on the farther seashore of the Red Sea that the Egyptian pursuers of the Israelites lay dead. It was when the people of God had genuinely undertaken the journey to the land which God had given them, that the grasp of their enemy gave way and the dead hands let them go. You may fight with your enemy on his own ground, only trying to get the immediate better of him, and win what he claims for yourself, and your fight will go on, more or less a failure, more or less a victory, forever. You must go forth into a new land, into the new ambition of a higher life, and then, when he tries to follow you there, he perishes.

O selfish man! not merely by trying not to be selfish, but by entering into the new joy of unselfish consecration, so only shall you kill your selfishness. When you are vigorously trying to serve your fellowmen, the last chance that you will be unjust or cruel to them will disappear. When you are full of enthusiasm for truth, the cold hands of falsehood will let you go. Get the Egyptian off his own ground, seek not the same low things by higher means; seek higher things, and the low means will know that they cannot hold you their slave. They will lie down and die. And then the pillar of fire and the pillar of cloud will have you for their own and lead you on in your free journey.

With regard, then, to a man's permanent escape from evil, may we not say these two things — that it must come about as the natural privilege of his life, and it must be positive? To the soul which has finally escaped from sin into the full freedom of the perfect life, the soul which has entered into the celestial liberty, must not these two things be clear — first that his old dream of life was a delusion, that he was never meant to be the thing which he so long allowed himself to be; and, second, that the great interests of the celestial life, the service of God which has there claimed the child of God, makes sure forever that there shall be no return to the old servitude? And what we dare to believe shall there in heaven come perfectly, and with reference to all wickedness, why may we not believe that here and now it may come in its degree with reference to some special sin? Know that it is not natural that you should steal, that you should lie; get rid of the first awful assumption that it is bound up with your constitution, cease to be a weak fatalist about it. That is the first thing. And then launch bravely forth into brave works of positive honesty and truth. Insist that your life shall not merely deny some falsehood, but that it shall assert some truth. Then, not till then, shall the lie let you go, and your soul count it impossible ever again to do — wonderful, almost incredible, that it ever should have done — what once it used to do from day to day.

31

I think that there are few things about our human nature which are more constantly marvellous than its power of acclimating itself in moral and spiritual regions where it once seemed impossible that it should live at all. The tree upon the hillside says: "Here and here alone can I live. Here my fathers lived in all their generations. Into this hard soil they struck their roots, and drank their sustenance out of its rocky depths. Take me down to the plain and I shall die." The gardener knows better. He takes the doubting and despairing plant and carries it, even against its will, to the broad valley, and sets it where the cold winds shall not smite it, and where the rich ground feeds it with luxuriance. And almost as they touch each other the ground and the root claim one another, and rich revelations of its own possibility flood the poor plant and fill it full of marvel with itself.

Of less and less consequence and meaning seem to me those easy things which men are always saying about their own natures and character. "I have no spiritual capacity," says one. "It is not in me to be a saint," another cries. "I have a covetous soul. I cannot live except in winning money." "I can make many sacrifices, but I cannot give up my drink." "I can do many things, but I cannot be reverent." So the man talks about himself. Poor creature, does he think that he knows, down to its center, this wonderful humanity of his? It all sounds so plausible and is so untrue! "Surely the man must know himself and his own limitations." Why must he? How can he know what lurking power lies packed away within the near-opened folds of this inactive life? Has he ever dared to call himself the child of God, and for one moment felt what that involves? Has he ever attacked the task which demands those powers whose existence he denies, or tried to press on into the region where those evil things cannot breathe which he complacently declares are an inseparable portion of his life? There is nothing on earth more seemingly significant and more absolutely insignificant than men's judgment of their own moral and spiritual limitations.

When the fallacy has been exposed, when the man has become something which he used to go about declaring that it was absolutely impossible that he should ever be, or has cast finally away that which he has counted a very part and portion of his life, it is often very interesting to see how he thinks of his cast-off sin. He, if he is a true man, counts his escape complete, but he never forgets his old bondage. He is always one whom God has led "out of the land of Egypt." Egypt is still there, although he has escaped from it. Egypt did not cease to be when the Egyptians with whom he had to do fell dead. Men are still doing the sin which has now become impossible for him. He understands those men by his past, while he cannot imagine himself sharing their life today. He is full of sympathy with the sinner, which is one with, of the same substance as, his security against the sin. Pity and hopefulness and humility and strength all blend into the peaceful and settled composure of his life.

It is a noble attitude towards a dead sin. You look into its dead face and are almost grateful to it. Not with a gratitude which makes you any way more tolerant of its character. You hate it with your heart — but look! Has it not given you self-knowledge, and made you cry out to God and set your face towards the new life?

My friends, get something done! Get something done! Do not go on forever in idle skirmishing with the same foe. Realize, as you sit here, who your chief enemy is, what vice of mind or body, what false or foul habit. Cry out to God for strength. Set your face resolutely to a new life in which that vice shall have no part. Go out and leave it dead. Plenty of new battles and new foes, but no longer that battle and that foe! Get something done! May He who overcame, not merely for Himself but for us all, give you courage and make you sharers in His victory and in the liberty which He attained.

# The Man of Macedonia

—ɱ—

*And a vision appeared unto Paul in the night. There stood a man of Macedonia, and prayed him, saying: Come over into Macedonia and help us.*

Acts xvi.9

It was the moment when a new work was opening before the great apostle; nothing less than the carrying of the Gospel into Europe. He had passed through Asia and was sleeping at Troas, with the Mediterranean waters sounding in his ears; and, visible across them, the islands which were the broken fringes of another continent. We cannot think that this was the first time that it had come into Paul's mind to think of christianizing Europe. We can well believe that on the past day he had stood and looked westward, and thought of the souls of men as hardly any man since him has known how to think of them, and longed to win for his Master the unknown world that lay beyond the waters. But now, in his sleep, a vision comes, and that completes whatever preparation may have been begun before, and in the morning he is ready to start.

And so it is that before every well-done work the vision comes. We dream before we accomplish. We start with the glorified image of what we are to do shining before our eyes, and it is its splendor that encourages and entices us through all the drudgery of the labor that we meet. The captain dreams out his battle sleeping in his tent. The quick and subtle-brained inventor has visions of his new wonder of machinery before the first toothed wheel is fitted to its place. You merchants see the great enterprise that is to make your fortune break out of vacancy and develop all its richness to you, as if it were a very inspiration from above. Nay, what is all our boyhood, that comes before our life, and thinks and pictures to itself what life shall be, that fancies and resolves and is impatient — what is it but just the vision before the work, the dream of Europe coming to many a young life, as it sleeps at Troas, on the margin of the sea? The visions before the work; it is their strength which conquers the difficulties, and lifts men up out of the failures, and redeems the tawdriness or squalidness of the labor that succeeds.

And such preparatory visions, the best of them, take the form and tone of importunate demands. The man hears the world crying out for just this thing which he is going to start to do tomorrow morning. This battle is to save the cause. This new invention is to turn the tide of wealth. This mighty bargain is to make trade another thing. The world must have it. And the long vision of boyhood is in the same strain too. There is something in him, this new boy says, which other men have never had. His new life has its own distinctive difference. He will fill some little unfilled necessary place. He will touch some little untouched spring. The world needs him. It may prove afterwards that the vision was not wholly true. It may seem as if, after all, only another duplicate life was added to a million others, which the world might very well have done without; but still the power of the vision is not soon exhausted, the mortifying confession is not made at once, and before it wholly fades away the vision gives a power and momentum to the life which the life never wholly loses.

And indeed we well may doubt whether the vision was a false one, even when the man himself, in his colder and less hopeful years, comes to think and say that it was. We well may doubt whether, with the infinite difference of personal life and character which God sends into the world, every true and earnest man has not some work that he alone can do, some place that he alone can fill; whether there is not somewhere a demand that he alone can satisfy; whether the world does not need him, is not calling to him, "Come and help us," as he used to hear it in the vision that was shown to him upon the seashore.

So much we say of preparatory visions in general. I want to look with you at this vision of Paul's, and see how far we can understand its meaning, and how much we can learn from it. A Macedonian comes before the apostle of Christ, and asks him for the gospel. The messenger is the representative, not of Macedonia only, but of all Europe. Macedonia is only the nearest country into which the traveller from Asia must cross first. There he stands in his strange dress, with his strange western look, with his strange gestures, before the waking or the sleeping Paul, begging in a strange language, which only the pentecostal power of spiritual appreciative sympathy can understand — "Come over and help us." But what was this Macedonia and this Europe which he represented? Did it want the gospel? Had it sent him out because it was restless and craving and uneasy, and could not be satisfied until it heard the truth about Jesus Christ, which Paul of Tarsus had to tell? Nothing of that kind whatsoever. Europe was going on perfectly contented in its heathenism. Its millions knew of nothing that was wanting to their happiness. They were full of their business and their pleasures, scheming for little self-advancements, taking care of their families, living in their tastes or their passions; a few questioning with themselves deep problems of perplexed philosophy, a few hanging votive wreaths on the cold altars of marble gods and goddesses, some looking upward and some downward and some inward for their life; but none looking eastward to where the apostle was sleeping, or, farther east, beyond him, to where the new sun of the new religion was making the dark sky bright with promise on that silent night. So far as we can know there was not one man in Macedonia who wanted Paul. When he went over there the next day, he found what? — a few bigoted Jews, some crazy soothsayers and witches, multitudes of indifferent heathen, a few open-hearted men and women who heard and believed what he had to tell them, but not one who had believed before, or wanted to believe — not one who met him at the ship and said, "Come, we have waited for you; we sent for you; we want your help." But what then means the man from Macedonia? If he was not the messenger of the Macedonians, who was he? Who sent him? Ah! there is just the key to it. God sent him. Not the Macedonians themselves. They did not want the gospel. God sent him, because He saw that they needed the

36

gospel. The mysterious man was an utterance not of the conscious want but of the unconscious need of those poor people. A heart and being of them, deeper and more essential than they knew themselves, took shape in some strange method by the power of God, and came and stood before the sleeping minister and said, "Come over and help us." The "man of Macedonia" was the very heart and essence of Macedonia, the profoundest capacities of truth and goodness and faith and salvation which Macedonia itself knew nothing of, but which were its real self. These were what took form and pleaded for satisfaction. It is not easy to state it; but look at Europe as it has been since, see the new life which has come forth, the profound spirituality, the earnest faith, the thoughtful devotion, the active unselfishness which has been the Europe of succeeding days; and then we may say that this, and more than this, all that is yet to come, was what God saw lying hidden and hampered, and set free to go and beg for help and release, from the disciple who held the key which has unlocked the fetters.

And is not this a very noble and a very true idea? It is the unsatisfied soul, the deep need, all the more needy because the outside life, perfectly satisfied with itself, does not know that it is needy all the time — it is this that God hears pleading. This soul is the true Macedonia. And so this, as the representative Macedonian, the man of Macedonia, brings the appeal. How noble and touching is the picture which this gives us of God. The unconscious needs of the world are all appeals and cries to Him. He does not wait to hear the voice of conscious want. The mere vacancy is a begging after fulness; the mere poverty is a supplication for wealth; the mere darkness cries for light. Think then a moment of God's infinite view of the capacities of His universe, and consider what a great cry must be forever going up into His ears to which His soul longs and endeavors to respond. Wherever any man is capable of being better or wiser or purer than he is, God hears the soul of that man crying out after the purity and wisdom and goodness which is its right, and of which it is being defrauded by the angry passions or the stubborn will. When you shut out any light or truth from your inner self, by the shutters of avarice or indolence which your outer, superficial, worldly self so easily slips up — that inner self, robbed, starved, darkened, not conscious of its want, hidden away there under the hard surface of your worldliness, has yet a voice which God can hear, accusing before Him your own cruelty to yourself. What a strong piteous wail of dissatisfaction must He hear from this world which seems so satisfied with itself. Wherever a nation is sunk in slavery or barbarism it cannot be so perfectly contented with its chains but that He hears the soul of it crying out after liberty and civilization. Wherever a man or a body of men is given to bigotry and prejudice, the love of darkness cannot be so complete but that He hears the human heart begging for the light that it was made for. Wherever lust is ruling, He hears the appeal of a hidden, outraged purity somewhere under the foul outside, and sends to it His help. Alas for us if God helped us only when we knew we needed Him and went to Him with full self-conscious wants! Alas for us if every need which we know not, had not a voice for Him and did not call Him to us! Did the world want the Savior? Was it not into a blindness so dark that it did not know that it was blind, into a wickedness so wicked that it was not looking for a Savior, that the Savior came? And when we look back can we say that we wanted the Lord who has taken us into His service and made us His children? Tell me, O Christian, was it a conscious want — was it not the cry of a silent need, that brought the Master to your side at first and so drew you to His? "He first loved us!" Our hope is in the ear which God has for simple need; so that mere emptiness cries out to Him for filling, mere poverty for wealth.

I cannot help turning aside a moment here just to bid you think what the world would be if men were like God in this respect. Suppose that we, all of us, heard every kind of need crying to us with an appeal which we could not resist. Out of every suffering and constraint and wrong, suppose there came to us, as out of Macedonia there came to Paul, a ghost, a vision, presenting at once to us the fact of need and the possibility of what the needy man might be if the need were satisfied and the chain broken. Suppose such visions came and stood around us crying out "Help us." You go through some wretched street and not a beggar touches your robe or looks up in your face, but the bare, dreadful presence of poverty cries out of every tumbling shanty and every ragged pretence of dress. You go among the ignorant, and out from under their contented ignorance their hidden power of knowledge utters itself and says "O teach us." It is not enough for you that the oppressed are satisfied with their oppression. That only makes you the more eager to feed into consciousness and strength that hunger after liberty which they are too degraded to feel. You see a sick man contented with dogged acquiescence and submission, and you want to show him the possibility and to lead him to the realization, of a resignation and delight in suffering which he never dreams of now. Mere pain is itself a cry for sympathy; mere darkness an appeal for light.

"Ah," do you say, "that must be a most uncomfortable way of living. The world forever clamoring for help! Those things are not my mission, not my work. If the world does not know its needs I will not tell it. Let it rest content. That is best for it"? But there have been, and, thank God, there are, men of a better stuff than you; men who cannot know of a need in all the world, from the need of a child fallen in the street, whose tears are to be wiped away, to the need of a nation lying in sin, whose wickedness must be rebuked to its face at the cost of the rebuker's life; there are men who cannot know of a need in all the world without its taking the shape of a personal appeal to them. They must go and do this thing. There are such men who seem to have a sort of magnetic attraction for all wrongs and pains. All grievances and woes fly to them to be righted and consoled. They attract need. They who cannot sleep at Troas but the soul of Macedonia finds them out and comes across and begs them "Come and help us." We all must be thankful to know that there are such men among us, however little we may feel that we are such men ourselves; nay, however little we may want to be such men.

But let us come a little nearer to the truth that we are studying. It seems to me that all which we have said about the man of Macedonia includes the real state of the case with reference to the essential need of the human soul for the Gospel. We often hear of the great cry of human nature for the truth of Christ, man craving the Savior. What does it mean? The world moves on and every face looks satisfied. Eating and drinking and working and studying, loving and hating, struggling and enjoying — those things seem to be sufficient for men's wants. There is no discontent that men will tell you of. They are not conscious of a need. I stop you, the most careless hearer in the church tonight, as you go out, and say "Are you satisfied?" and honestly you answer "Yes! My business and my family, they are enough for me"; "Do you feel any need of Christ?" and honestly you answer "No! Sometimes I fear that it will go ill with me by and by, if I do not seek Him, but at present I do not want Him; I do not see how I should be happier if I had Him here." That is about the honest answer which your heart would make. But what then? Just as below the actual Macedonia which did not care for Paul nor want him, there was another possible, ideal Macedonia which God saw and called forth and sent in a visionary form to beg the help it could not do without, so to that civil flippant answerer of my question at the church door I could say: "Below this outer self of yours which is satisfied with family and business, there is another self which you know nothing of but which God sees, which He values as your truest and deepest self, which to His sight is a real person pleading so piteously for help that He has not been able to resist its pleading, but has sent His ministers, has sent His Bible — nay, has come Himself to satisfy it with that spiritual aid it cannot do without." I can imagine a look of perplexity and wonder, a turning back, an inward search for this inner self, a strange, bewildered doubt whether it exists at all.

And yet, this coming forth of inner selves with their demands, is it not the one method of all progress? What does it mean when a slave, long satisfied with being fed and housed and clothed, some day comes to the knowledge that he was meant to be free, and can rest satisfied as a slave no longer? What is it when the savage's inner nature is touched by the ambition of knowledge, and he cannot rest until he grows to be a scholar? What is it when a hard, selfish man's crust is broken, and a sensitive, tender soul uncovered, which makes life a wretched thing to him from that moment, unless he has somebody besides himself to love and help and cherish? These men would not believe an hour before that such appetites and faculties were in them; but God knew them, and heard them all the time; and long before the men dreamed of it themselves, the slave was crying out to Him for freedom, and the savage for culture, and the tyrant for love. Now is it strange that, also unknown to you, there should be other appetites and faculties in you which need a satisfaction? The Bible says there are. Experience says there are. Let us see if we can find some of them.

40

1. The first need is a God to love and worship. Anybody who looks wisely back into history sees, I think, regarding man's need of a God to love and worship, just what I have stated to be true. Not that man was always seeking God, or always miserable, when he did not find Him. One sees multitudes of men, and sometimes whole periods, or whole countries, that seem to have no sense of want whatever, to have settled down into the purest materialism and the most utter self-content. But he sees also indications everywhere that the need was present, even where the want was not felt. He sees the idea of God keeping a sort of persistent foothold in the human heart, which proves to him that it belongs there; that, whether the heart wants it or not, it and the heart are mates, made for one another, and so tending towards each other by a certain essential gravitation, whatever accidental causes may have tried to produce an estrangement between them. Take one such indication only, a very striking one, I think. There is in man a certain power of veneration, of awe, of adoration. This has always showed itself. In all sorts of men, in all sorts of places, it has broken out; and men have tried to adapt it to all sorts of objects, to satisfy it with all sorts of food. The idolater has offered to his faculty of reverence his wooden idol, and said "There, worship that"; the philosopher has offered it his abstract truth, and said "Venerate that"; the philanthropist has offered it his ideal humanity, and said "Worship that"; and one result has always followed. Everywhere where nothing higher than the idol, the theory, or the humanity was offered for the reverence to fasten on, everywhere where it was offered no one supreme causal God, not merely the object of reverence has ceased to be reverenced, but the very power of reverence itself has been dissipated and lost; and idolatry, philosophy, philanthropy alike have grown irreverent, and man has lost and often come to despise that faculty of venerating and submissive awe, the awe of love, for which he found no use. If this be true, that there is a faculty in man which dies out on any other food, and thrives only on the personal Deity, then have we not exactly what I tried to describe, a need of which one may be utterly unconscious, and yet which is no less a need, crying, though the man does not hear it, for supply?

This is precisely the ground which I would take with any thoughtful man who told me seriously and without flippancy that he felt no want of God, that he felt no lack in the absence of relations between his life and that of a supreme infinite Father. "Yes," I would say, "but there is in you a power of loving awe which needs infinite perfection and mercy to call it out and satisfy it. There is an affection which you cannot exercise towards any imperfect being. It is that mixture of admiration and reverence and fear and love, which we call worship. Now ask yourself, Are you not losing the power of worship? Is it not dying for want of an object? Are you not conscious that a power of the soul, which other men use, which you used once perhaps, is going from you? Are you not substituting critical, carefully limited, philosophical, partial approbations of imperfect men and things, for that absolute, unhindered, whole-souled outpouring of worship which nothing but the perfect can demand or justify? If this power is not utterly to die within you, do you not need God? If you are not to lose that highest reach of love and fear where, uniting, they make worship, must you not have God? Lo! before this expiring faculty the personal God comes and stands, and it lifts up its dying hands to reach after Him; it opens its dying eyes to look upon Him; as when a man is perishing of starvation, the sight of bread summons him back to life. He need not die, but live, for here is his own life-food come to him."

Woe to the man who loses the faculty of worship, the faculty of honoring and loving and fearing not merely something better than himself, but something which is the absolute best, the perfect good — his God! The life is gone out of his life when this is gone. There is a cloud upon his thought, a palsy on his action, a chill upon his love. Because you must worship, therefore you must have God.

2. But more than this. Every man needs not merely a God to worship, but also, taking the fact which meets us everywhere of an estrangement by sin between mankind and God, every man needs some power to turn him and bring him back; some reconciliation, some Reconciler, some Savior for his soul. Again I say he may not know his need, but none the less the need is there. But, if a man has reached the first want and really is desiring God, then I think he generally does know, or in some vague way suspect, this second want, and does desire reconciliation. It is so natural! Two of you, who have been friends, have quarrelled. Your very quarrel, it may be, has brought out to each of you how

much you need each other. You never knew your friend was so necessary to your comfort and your happiness. You cannot do without him. Then at once, "How shall I get to him?" becomes your question. O the awkwardness and difficulty, the stumbling and shuffling and blundering of such efforts at return. Men are afraid and ashamed to try. They do not know how they will be received. They cannot give up their old pride. Rebellious tempers and bad habits block the way. I doubt not, so frequent are they, that there are people here tonight who are stumbling about in some such bog of unsettled quarrel, longing to get back to some friend whom they value more in their disagreement than even in the old days of unbroken peace. Their whole soul is hungering for reconciliation. The misery of their separation is that each at heart desires what neither has the frankness and the courage to attain.

Now under all outward rebellion and wickedness, there is in every man who ought to be a friend of God, and that means every man whom God has made, a need of reconciliation. To get back to God, that is the struggle. The soul is Godlike and seeks its own. It wants its Father. There is an orphanage, a homesickness of the heart which has gone up into the ear of God, and called the Savior, the Reconciler, to meet it by His wondrous life and death. I, for my part, love to see in every restlessness of man's moral life everywhere, whatever forms it takes, the struggles of this imprisoned desire. The reason may be rebellious, and vehemently cast aside the whole story of the New Testament, but the soul is never wholly at its rest away from God. Does this not put it most impressively before us? Is it not something at least to startle us and make us think, if we come to know that the very God of heaven saw a want, a struggle, a longing of our souls after Himself, which was too deep, too obscure, too clouded over with other interests for even us to see ourselves, and came to meet that want with the wonderful manifestation of the incarnation, the atonement? We hear of the marvellous power of the Gospel, and we come to doubt it when we see the multitudes of unsaved men. But it is true. The Gospel is powerful, omnipotent. A truth like this, thoroughly believed, and taken in, must melt the hardest heart and break down the most stubborn will. It does not save men, simply because it is not taken in, not believed. The Gospel is powerless, just as the medicine that you keep corked in its vial on the shelf is powerless. If you will not take it, what matters it what marvellous drugs have lent their subtle virtues to it? Believe and thou art saved. Understand and know, and thoroughly take home into your affection and your will, the certain truth that Christ saw your need of Him when you did not know it yourself, and came to help you at a cost past all calculation — really believe this and you must be a new man and be saved.

3. I should like to point out another of the needs of man which God has heard appealing to Him and has satisfied completely. I know that I must speak about it very briefly. It is the need of spiritual guidance; and it is a need whose utterance not God's ear alone can hear. Every man hears it in the race at large, and hears it in his brethren, however deaf he may be to it in himself. I think there never was a materialist so complete that he did not realize that the great mass of men were not materialists, but believed in spiritual forces and longed for spiritual companies. He might think the spiritual tendency the wildest of delusions, but he could not doubt its prevalence. How could he? Here is the whole earth full of it. Language is all shaped upon it. Thought is all saturated with it. In the most imposing and the most vulgar methods, by solemn oracles and rocking tables, men have been always trying to put themselves into communication with the spiritual world and to get counsel and help from within the vale. And if we hear the cry from one another, how much more God hears it. Do you think, poor stumbler, that God did not know it when you found no man to tell you what you ought to do in a perplexity which, as it rose around you, seemed, as it was, unlike any bewilderment that had ever puzzled any man before? Do you think, poor sufferer, that God did not hear it when in your sickness and pain men came about you with their kindness, fed you with delicacies, and spread soft cushions under the tortured body, and all the time the mind diseased, feeling so bitterly that these tender cares for the body's comfort did not begin to touch its spiritual pain, lay moaning and wailing out its hopeless woe? Do you think now, my brother, when you have got a hard duty to do, a hard temptation to resist; when you have felt all about you for strength, called in prudence and custom and respectability and interest to keep you straight, and found them all fail because, by their very nature, they have no spiritual strength to give; when now you stand just ready to give way and fall,

ready to go tomorrow morning and do the wrong thing that you have struggled against so long — do you think that God does not know it all, and does not hear the poor frightened soul's cry for help against the outrage that is threatening her, and has not prepared a way of aid? The power of the Holy Spirit! — an everlasting spiritual presence among men. What but that is the thing we want? That is what the old oracles were dreaming of, what the modern spiritualists tonight are fumbling after. The power of the Holy Ghost by which every man who is in doubt may know what is right, every man whose soul is sick may be made spiritually whole, every weak man may be made a strong man — that is God's one sufficient answer to the endless appeal of man's spiritual life; that is God's one great response to the unconscious need of spiritual guidance, which he hears crying out of the deep heart of every man.

I hope that I have made clear to you what I mean. I would that we might understand ourselves, see what we might be; nay, see what we are. While you are living a worldly and a wicked life, letting all sacred things go, caring for no duty, serving no God, there is another self, your possibility, the thing that you might be, the thing that God gave you a chance to be; and that self, wronged and trampled on by your recklessness, escapes and flies to God with its appeal: "O, come and help me. I am dying. I am dying. Give me Thyself for Father. Give me Thy Son for Savior. Give me Thy Spirit for my guide." So your soul pleads before God; pleads with a pathos all the more piteous in his ears, because you do not hear the plea yourself; pleads with such sacred prevalence that the great merciful Heart yields and gives all that the dumb appeal has asked.

What does it mean? Here is the Gospel in its fulness. Here is God for you to worship. Here is Christ to save you. Here is the Comforter. Have you asked for them, my poor careless brother, that here they stand with such profusion of blessing, waiting to help you? "Ah, no," you say, "I never asked." Suppose, when Paul landed in Macedonia, he had turned to the careless group who watched him as he stepped ashore, and said, "Here am I; you sent for me. Here am I with the truth, the Christ you need" — what must their answer have been? "O, no, you are mistaken; we never sent; we do not know you; we do not want you!"

Yet they had sent. Their needs had stood and begged him to come over, out of the lips of that mysterious man of Macedonia. And when they came to know this, they must have found all the more precious the preciousness of a Gospel which had come to them in answer to a need they did not know themselves.

And so your needs have stood, they are standing now before God. They have moved Him to deep pity and care for you. And He has sent the supply for them before you knew you wanted it. And here it is — a God to worship, a Savior to believe in, a Comforter to rest upon. O, if you ever do come, as I would to God that you might come tonight, to take this mercy, and let your thirsty soul drink of this water of life! then you will feel most deeply the goodness which provided for you before you even knew that you needed any such provision; then you will understand those words of Paul: "God commendeth His love toward us, in that while we were yet sinners Christ died for us."

Till that time comes, what can God do but stand and call you and warn you and beg you to know yourself. "Because thou sayest, I am rich and increased with goods, and have need of nothing, and knowest not that thou art wretched and miserable and poor and blind and naked, I counsel thee to buy of Me gold tried in the fire, that thou mayest be rich. Behold, I stand at the door and knock. If any man hear My voice, and open the door, I will come in and sup with him, and he with Me."

# The Withheld Completions of Life

—⁓—

*Peter said unto Him, Lord, why cannot I follow Thee now?*

John xiii.37

It is from passages like this that we have all gathered our impression
of St. Peter's character, an impression probably clearer and more
correct than we have with regard to any other of the Lord's disciples.
Here is all his impulsiveness and affection, the unreasonableness and
impatience which still excite our admiration and our love because they
strike the note of a deeper and diviner reason, of which the prudent
people seldom come in sight. They were sitting together at the Last
Supper. Jesus had just told his friends that He must leave them. Simon
Peter was the first to leap forward with the question, "Lord, whither
goest Thou?" Jesus replied, "Whither I go thou canst not follow me
now, but thou shalt follow me afterwards." There was the promise of a
future companionship between the disciple and the Master, which was
to carry on and complete the companionship of the past, whose preciousness was now coming out as it drew near its close. There opened
before the loving man a mysterious but beautiful prospect of some
more perfect paths through which he might walk with Jesus, and find
the completion of that intercourse of which the well-remembered
walks through the streets of Jerusalem and the lanes of Galilee had
been only the promise. The keen joy of dying with his Lord seemed all
that was needed to finish the joy of living with Him; and when he sees

47

all this deferred, when Christ is, as it seems, gathering up His robes to walk alone into the experience that lies before Him, Peter breaks out in a cry of impatience, "Why cannot I follow Thee *now?*" The life with Jesus, which is the only life for him, seems to be passing hopelessly away. The promise of a future day when it shall be restored to him does not satisfy him; indeed it hardly seems to take hold of him at all. He wants it now. It was unreasonable. So it is unreasonable when by the side of your friend's grave you wish that you could die and enter at once upon the everlasting companionship. So it is unreasonable when, as your friend goes alone into a cloud of sorrow, the sunlight of prosperity in which you are left standing seems hateful to you, and you grudge him his solitary pain. How unreasonable Peter was appeared only a few hours later, when his denial proved his unfitness to go with Jesus into the mystery and pain which He was entering. It is an unreasonable impatience, but it is one that makes us love and honor the unreasonable man, and adds a new pleasure to the study of all Peter's after-life, as we watch him treading more and more in his Lord's footsteps, and at last really following his Lord into His glory.

It has seemed to me as if this verse opened a great subject, one which is continually pressing upon us, one that is full of practical bewilderments; a subject that must come home to the thoughts of many of the people in this congregation. That subject is, The Withheld Completions of Life. St. Peter felt dimly that the life of Jesus was opening into something so large that all which had gone before would be seen to have been only the vestibule and preparation for what was yet to come. He vaguely felt that this death, in whose shadow they were sitting, was the focus into which all the lines along which they had travelled were converging only that they might open into larger and more wonderful fields of experience. And just then, when his expectation was keenest, when his love was most eager, an iron curtain fell across his view. "Whither I go thou canst not follow me now," said Jesus. The completion was withheld. The life of Jesus was broken off, and they who had lived with Him were left standing bewildered and distressed in front of the mystery which hid Him from their sight.

And that is what is always happening; what it is so hard for us to understand and yet what we must understand, or life is all a puzzle. For all our life has its tendencies. It would be intolerable to us if we could not trace tendencies in our life. If everything stood still, or if things only moved round in a circle, it would be a dreary and a dreadful thing to live. But we rejoice in life because it seems to be carrying us somewhere; because its darkness seems to be rolling on towards light, and even its pain to be moving onward to a hidden joy. We bear with incompleteness, because of the completion which is prophesied and hoped for. But it is the delay of that completion, the way in which when we seem to be all ready for it, it does not come, the way in which, when we seem to be just on the brink of it, the iron curtain drops across our path; this is what puzzles and distresses us. The tendency that is not allowed to reach the fulfillment which alone gave it value seems a mockery. You watch your plant growing, and see its wonderful building of the woody fibre, its twining of the strong roots, its busy life-blood hurrying along its veins. The dignity and beauty of the whole process is in the completion which it all expects. Some morning you step into your garden and the deep-red flower is blazing full-blown on the stem, and all is plain. The completion has justified the process. But suppose the plant to have been all the time conscious of the coming flower, to have felt its fire already in the tumultuous sap, and yet to have felt itself held back from blossoming. Not today! not today! each morning as it tried to crown itself with the glory toward which all its tendencies had struggled. Would it not be a very puzzled and impatient and unhappy little plant, as it stood wondering why its completion was withheld, and what delayed its flower?

Now there are certain conditions which are to all good life just what the flower is to the plant. They furnish it its natural completion. They crown its struggles with a manifest success. There are certain fine results of feeling and contentment which are the true and recognized results of the best ways of living. They crown the hidden resolutions and the prosaic struggles of men with beautiful conclusiveness, as the gorgeous flower finishes all that the buried root and the rugged stalk of the plant have done, and make it a perfect and satisfactory thing. The flower is the plant's success. These conditions of peace and pleasure are the life's success in the same way, but when the life, conscious of the character in itself out of which these conditions ought to come,

49

finds that they do not come, finds that it pauses on the brink of its completion and cannot blossom, then comes bewilderment; then come impatient questionings and doubts. This is the state of many lives, I think, especially about religious things. I want to speak with you of this, and see if we can get any light upon it.

But lest I speak too vaguely, let me take special instances. In that way we can understand it best; and here is the first, perhaps the simplest. Suppose we have a man thoroughly, genuinely, unselfishly devoted to the good of fellow-men. It is not so uncommon as we think. It matters not upon what scale the self-devotion may take place. A poor obscure woman in a sick-room giving her days and nights, her health and strength, to some poor invalid; or a great brilliant man out in the world neglecting his personal interests in the desire that some of the lagging causes of God may be helped forward, or that the men of the city may be better clothed and fed and housed. Now such a life, in whatever scale it may be lived, has its legitimate completion. There is one natural and healthy result to which it is all tending, one flower into whose beauty its hard work was made to bloom. The natural flower which should crown that life of self-devotion is men's gratitude. The joyous, thankful recognition of your fellow-men is the true issue of the life which gives itself for them. Perhaps in ringing cheers that make the world stand still to listen, perhaps only in the weak, silent pressure of the hand, or the last feeble lighting of the eyes, with which he whose sick-bed you have watched thanks you unutterably just as he dies; some way or other, thanks is the completion of service. The two belong together, service and thanks; not in the way of bargain, not by deliberate arrangement, but in the very nature of the things. The man who does no good expects no thanks. The selfish life feels and shows the unnaturalness if men make a mistake and lavish their gratitude upon it. It is as if men tied the glorious flower on to the top of a wooden post that has no germinating power. But to the life that serves, the gratitude that recognizes service belongs as the warmth belongs to the sunlight, or the echo to the sound. And now suppose that the gratitude does not come. Your friend turns his face to the wall and dies, and never looks at you. The people pass you by, and waste their cheers upon some charlatan who has been working for himself. What then? Is there no disappointment of the soul; no sense of a withheld completion; no consciousness of something wrong, of something that falls short of the complete and rounded issue which was natural? Indeed there is! "What does it mean?" you ask with wonder, even with impatience.

And in answer to your wondering question there are two things to be said. The first is this: that such a suspension of the legitimate result, this failure of the flower to complete the plant, does show beyond all doubt a real condition of disorder. The natural result of your self-devotion has not come because the state of things in which you live is unnatural. That must be recognized. There is a reason in your wonder and surprise. Something is wrong. If you let your surprise appear, if men can see, as they look into your face, pain and bewilderment at their ingratitude, no doubt they will misunderstand you. They will laugh and jeer. They will cry, "Oh, after all, then, you were not unselfish; you did this thing not for us, but to be seen of men and to be thanked. It is good enough for you not to get it if that was what you wanted." But it may very well be that they are wrong; you were unselfish; you did not work for thanks. When the thanks do not come it is not your loss, it is the deranged, disordered state of things which the world shows that troubles you. When Jesus wept over ungrateful Jerusalem, did He not feel its ingratitude? But was it not the disturbed world where such ingratitude was possible, and not any mere loss of recognition of Himself, which lay at the bottom of His grief? When your child is ungrateful to you, is it the neglect of yourself, or is it not the deranged family, the broken and demoralized home, that saddens you? It is the violation of a deep, true instinct. I think that this is always on Christ's soul. The world's ingratitude to Him showed Him how wrong the world was. In a perfect world every tendency must open to its result. Its Christ must be greeted with hosannas. They who receive His blessings must give Him their praise. The world is broken and disordered, that is the first thing that is meant when you help men and they scorn you, when the world's benefactors are neglected or despised.

But let us never think that we have reached all the meaning when we have reached that. Because any state of things is unnatural, it does not prove that there can come out of it no blessing. God very often leaves the consequences of a man's sins untouched, but in the midst of them makes it possible for His servant to live all the better life by the very derangements and distortions by which he is surrounded. So it is here. The service that a man does to his fellow-men does not bring down their gratitude upon him. And what then? There is a blessing which may come to him even out of the withholding of the legitimate completion of his service. It may throw him back upon the nature of the act itself, and compel him to find his satisfaction there. Many a man who, having served his brethren in public or in private, has looked up from his work with a true human longing that his work should be recognized, and heard no sound of gratitude, has then retreated to the self-sacrifice itself and found, in the mere doing of that, an even deeper, even keener joy than he could have gathered from the most spontaneous and hearty thanks. That has been the support, the inner triumph of many a despised reformer and misunderstood friend. Men have found a joy which they could not have had in a world undisturbed, and whose moral order was perfect. The essence of any act is more and finer than its consequences are. It is better to live in the essence of an act than in its consequences or rewards. The consequences of an act are meant to interpret and manifest its essence; but if at any time the withholding of its consequence can drive us home more deep into its essence, is it not a blessing?

I think we cannot doubt that Christ's life manifested the essential and eternal joy of serving God, the dignity and beauty of helping man, as it could not have done if it had been heralded by the trumpets and followed by the cheers of human gratitude. Because He was "despised and rejected of men," we are able to see more clearly how truly He was His Father's "well-beloved Son." And if, as it may be, you, with no morbidness, no self-conceit, no querulousness, know that you have been helping some man, or some hundred men, from whom you get no gratitude — the manly thing for you to do in that withholding of the natural completion of your life is just what Christ did: first own that the world is out of order, and do not look with any certain confidence for a recognition which could be certain only in a world of moral perfectness; and then let its withholding drive you home to the blessedness of the service of other men in and for itself, recognized or unrecognized, thanked or unthanked, and to companionship with God, who understands it all.

As we come into the regions of more truly spiritual experience this truth of the withheld completions of life becomes more striking, and often much more puzzling. As we come to that history which goes on within a man's own heart, and where the action of other men does not intrude, it seems more strange that each cause cannot produce its full effect, and each growth blossom to its appointed flower. But even here I think that if we keep in mind the two considerations which I have been speaking of we shall find in them, if not the sufficient explanations, at least the supporting consolations of the withheld completions of our life. Look, for instance, at the connection of duty and happiness. Happiness is the natural flower of duty. The good man ought to be a thoroughly bright and joyous man. This is no theoretical conviction. It is the first quick instinct of the human heart. We do not know, I think, how deep in us lies this assurance that goodness and happiness belong together, how impossible it would be to take it out of us without deranging all our life. Just think, if there were no such assurance, what a dreadful thing happiness would be in the world. If to be happy meant nothing, or meant badness, if it had no connection with being good, how a laugh in the street would be dreadful to us, and the look of a bright, gay, happy face would strike upon our conscience like a cloud that sweeps across the sun. But no. From the innocence of childhood uttering itself in the child's sunny joy, on through the whole of life, there runs one constant conviction that goodness and happiness belong together. That conviction meets a thousand contradictions, but it is too strong for them all. It runs like a mountain stream along a course all blocked with rocks of difficulty; but none of them can permanently hinder it or turn it back. It slips under or around them all, this deep and live conviction that the tendency of goodness is to happiness. In this conviction lies the poetry of human life. This conviction has planted the Edens which all races have discerned behind them, and painted the Heavens which they have all seen before them. It is bound up with all belief in God. To cease to believe it would be to bow down at the footstool of a devil or a chance, and which of these would be the most terrible master who can say? With this conviction strong in us we come to some man's life — a life which we are sure is good; to call it wicked is to confuse all our idea of wickedness and goodness. And that life is all gloomy. Duty is done day after day, but done in utter dreariness; there is no smile upon the face, no ring of laughter in the voice; a good man, a just and pure man, a man who hates sin and whom you would not dare to think of tempting, and yet a sad man, not a glad man; a man to whom life is a burden, not an exhilaration and a joy. Such men there are; good without gladness, shocking and perplexing our deep certainty that to be good and to be glad belong together. To them we want to bring the two considerations which I dwelt on when I was speaking of self-sacrifice and gratitude. To recognize that it is unnatural, and so to struggle against it, not to yield to it, and yet, while it must last, to get what blessing we can out of it, by letting it drive us down deeper for our joy and comfort, into the very act and fact of doing righteousness, that is all that we can do, and that is enough to do when the golden link is broken and doing righteousness does not blossom into being happy. "I am trying to do right," a man says, "and yet the world is all dark to me; what can you say to me? Will you tell me still that there is a natural connection between doing right and being happy?" Surely I will, I answer. I will insist on your remembering it. I will warn you never to forget it, nor to get to counting gloominess the natural air and atmosphere of duty. I will beg you never to think it right, that when you are trying to be good you should still be unhappy. You must struggle against it. And yet, you must let the very fact that the connection can be broken prove to you that while the union of duty and joy is natural it is not essential and unbreakable. The plant ought to come to flower, but if the plant fails of its flower it is still a plant. The duty should open into joy, but it may fail of joy and still be duty. If the joy is not there, still hold the duty, and be sure that you have the real thing while you are holding that. Be all the more dutiful, though it be in the dark. Do righteousness and forget happiness, and so it is most likely that happiness will come. This is all that one can say, and this is enough to say. It will help the man neither despondently to submit to nor frantically to rebel against the unnatural postponement of the happiness which belongs to his struggle to do right. It will help him to be hopeful without impatience, and patient without despair.

But take another case, that comes still more distinctly within the limits of Christian experience. There are promises in the Bible, many of them, which declare that dedication to God shall bring communion with God. "Draw near to me and I will draw near to you," says God. And even without the special promise, that whole revelation of God which the Bible gives us involves such a necessity. It cannot be that a God all love surrounds us with His life, presses upon us, waits for us on every side, and yet the meanest soul can really turn to Him and throw itself open before Him, and not receive Him into its life. And yet sometimes the man does give himself to God, and the promise seems to fail. The heart draws near to God in conscious dedication, and it seems as if no answering communion came. The soul is laid upon the altar, and no hand of fire is seen reached out from heaven to take it up in love. Day follows day, year follows year, it may be, and the man given to God trembles when he hears other men talk of the joy of divine communion, because no such ever comes to him. Once more, to such a soul, to any such soul which is here today, there are the same two messages to bring. Never, no matter how long such exclusion from the presence of God may seem to last, though it go on year after year and you are growing old in your seeming orphanhood; never accept it, never make up your mind to it that it is right; never cease to expect that the doors will fly open and you will be admitted to all the joy of your Father's felt love and of unhindered communion with Him. Never lose out of your soul's sight the seat which is set for you in the very sanctuary of divine love. And what beside? Seek even more deeply the satisfaction which is in your consecration itself; and that you may find it, consecrate yourself more and more completely. Oh, it may well be that there are some of you who are listening intently at this moment, thinking perhaps that now, after a thousand disappointments in a thousand sermons, you may hear the word you need, which shall explain this terrible separation from your Father, which, while you give yourselves with all your souls to Him, still keeps you shut out from His communion. I cannot tell you all you want to know. Nobody can. But there are two great anxieties which I do feel for such a soul as yours. One is, lest you should give up hoping for and expecting that privilege of communion which, however long it be delayed, because you are a child of God is certainly yours in possibility, and must certainly be yours some day in possession. The other is, lest, since the consecration has not brought you the communion, you should think that the consecration is unreal, and so lose the power to be blessed by it, and the impulse to increase it. Christ has led you with Him thus far up to the line where you have given yourself to Him. Before you open the fields where you see the privilege of having His fulness given to you. But something seems to come across and shut you out from them. No wonder that you lift up a cry almost of bitterness: "Why cannot I follow thee now? Why this delay of the divinest life? Why so much duty with so little strength? Why only the journey and the hunger and the thirst, without the brook of refreshment by the way?" No man can wholly answer these questions, but multitudes of saints, if they could speak, would tell you how in their hindered lives God kept them true to such experience as they had attained: and so it was that, by and by, either before or after the great enlightenment of death, the hindrance melted away, and they who had been crying for years, "Lord, why cannot we follow Thee now?" passed forth into the multitude of those who follow the Lamb "whithersoever He goeth."

There is one other of the withheld completions of life of which I should like to speak, and only one. Among Christ's promises there is none that is dearer to one class of minds, minds of a very pure and noble character, than that which He spoke one day when He was in discussion with the Jews in the Temple. "If any man wills to do my will," He said, "he shall know of the doctrine, whether it be of God or whether I speak of myself." I have been struck by seeing how favorite a text that has become in our day. Many minds have rested upon it. Many earnest seekers after truth, bewildered by the difficulties of doctrine, almost ready to give up in despair have welcomed this declaration of the Lord, and gone out with new hope, that by the dedication of their wills, by trying to become obedient to Christ, they should come to understand the Christ who was so dark to them. Many and many a soul has found that that was indeed the message that it needed. Turning away from vain disputes of words, leaving theological subtleties alone, just trying to turn what it knew of Christ into a life, it has found — what He promised — that it has become assured of His divinity, sure that His doctrine was of God. Such souls have not found that the thousand curious questions of theology were answered, and all the mystery rolled away out of the sky of truth. Christ did not promise that. But

they have found what He did promise: that coming near to Him in obedience, they have been made sure of the true divinity that was in Him
and in the teachings that He gave. Such testimony comes abundantly
from all the ages, and from many souls today. It is not strange. It is like
all Christ's teachings — one utterance of an essential universal truth.
Everywhere the flower of obedience is intelligence. Obey a man with
cordial loyalty and you will understand him. Obey Jesus with cordial
loyalty and you will understand Jesus. Not by studying Him, but by doing His will, shall you learn how divine He is. Obedience completes itself in understanding.

And now are there any of us from whom that completion seems to
have been withheld? Are there any of us who, trying hard to do the
Lord's will wherever He has made it known to them, looking for it continually, are yet distressed to know that their Lord's nature has not become all clear to them? They must be sure, first, that they are right;
sure that Christ has not done for them what He promised, though He
may not have done what they chose to expect. They must be sure that
they have not really come to an essential faith that the doctrine of Jesus
is divine. To many souls that faith has come, while, bewildered still by
various forms of expression, they cannot even recognize their own belief. They must be sure again that their will to serve Christ has been indeed true; not simply the trying of an experiment from which they still
reserved the liberty to withdraw, but the unreserved and total dedication of themselves to Him. And what then? Sure of all this, still the
darkness and the doubts remain. Then they must come, it seems to me,
to the two principles which I have enforced this morning. Then they
must say to themselves: "This is unnatural; it ought not to be. My service, my true will-dedication ought to bring me out into the light; at
least I will remember that. I will not be content with darkness. I will not
let despair of positive belief settle down on me with its chilling power. I
will not rest until my service of Christ completes itself in the knowledge of Christ; and yet all the time while I am waiting I will find joy in
the service of Him, however dimly I may apprehend Him. I will find
deeper and deeper satisfaction in doing His will, though it be in the
midst of many doubts, though I be sorely puzzled when men ask me to
give my account of Him. It may be that just because obedience is not

able at once to complete itself in knowledge, the pure joy and deep culture which are in obedience itself may come to me more really and more richly." That is no barren lesson, my dear friends, to come to any man. You would not find it a barren lesson if it could come to you today. If to your life, struggling in obedience to Christ, but not able to clear itself into light about Christ, there could come, as from the Christ you long for, a command to you to struggle on still in hope because you must reach the light some day; and yet a command, while the light is withheld, to find satisfaction and growth in the ever-deepening struggle, would not that be the command you need? Oh that in His name I could utter this message to any souls who are thus trying to do His will, and yet seeming not to know His doctrine! Oh that I could bid them with His voice to persevere because there is light ahead, and yet to be thankful even now for the culture of the darkness! "Whither I go thou canst not follow me now, but thou shalt follow me afterwards." "Watch, therefore!"

I hope, then, that I have made clear this story of the withheld completions of our human life. The plant grows on toward its appointed flower, but before the blossom comes some hand is laid upon it, and the day of its blossoming is delayed. I have dwelt on a few illustrations, but the truth is everywhere. The emotional and affectional conditions are the natural flower of the wills and dedications of our life. But we resolve, we dedicate ourselves, and, though the prophecy and hope immediately begin to assert themselves all through us, the joy, the peace, the calmness of assurance, does not come. We are like southern plants, taken up to a northern climate and planted in a northern soil. They grow there, but they are always failing of their flowers. The poor exiled shrub dreams by a native longing of a splendid blossom which it has never seen, but is dimly conscious that it ought somehow to produce. It feels the flower which it has not strength to make in the half chilled but still genuine juices of its southern nature. That is the way in which the ideal life, the life of full completions, haunts us all. Nothing can really haunt us except what we have the beginning of, the native capacity for, however hindered, in ourselves. The highest angel does not tempt us because he is of another race from us; but God is our continual incitement because we are His children. So the ideal life is in our blood, and never will be still. We feel the thing we ought to be beating beneath the thing we are. Every time we see a man who has attained our human ideal a little more fully than we have, it wakens our languid blood and fills us with new longings. When we see Christ, it is as if a new live plant out of the southern soil were brought suddenly in among its poor stunted, transplanted brethren, and, blossoming in their sight, interpreted to each of them the restlessness and discontent which was in each of their poor hearts. When, led by Christ, we see God, it is as if the stunted, flowerless plants grew tall enough to stand up and look across all the miles that lie between, and see the glory of the perfect plant as it blooms in unhindered luxuriance in its southern home. And when we die and go to God, it is as if at last the poor shrub were plucked up out of its exile and taken back and set where it belonged, in the rich soil, under the warm sun, where the patience which it had learned in its long waiting should make all the deeper and richer the flower into which its experience was set free to find its utterance.

Patience and struggle. An earnest use of what we have now, and, all the time, an earnest discontent until we come to what we ought to be. Are not these what we need — what in their rich union we could not get, except in just such a life as this with its delayed completions? Jesus does not blame Peter when he impetuously begs that he may follow Him now. He bids him wait and he shall follow Him some day. But we can see that the value of his waiting lies in the certainty that he shall follow, and the value of his following, when it comes, will lie in the fact that he has waited. So, if we take all Christ's culture, we are sure that our life on earth may get already the inspiration of the heaven for which we are training, and our life in heaven may keep forever the blessing of the earth in which we were trained.

# A Whitsunday Sermon

—m—

*And they said unto him: We have not so much as heard
whether there be any Holy Ghost.*

Acts xix.2

It is always strange to us to find other people entirely ignorant of
what makes the whole interest of our own life. We can hardly understand how it is possible that men should live along year after year, it
may be generation after generation, knowing nothing about what
really makes life for us. If we did not have this or that resource we
should die, we should not care to live. Here is a man who has it not, and
yet his life seems to be worth a great deal to him. He goes on bright and
contented. Apply this to your love of reading. What would it be to you
if every book were shut? What would you do if all communication with
great minds through literature were broken off, if all the stimulus
which comes to your own mind were stopped? And yet there are plenty
of these men whom you meet every day who never open a book! Or
take the exercise of charity. You would find little pleasure in life perhaps if you were shut in on yourself and could do nothing for anybody
else. At least there are people of whom that is true. To find some one
whom you can help, and have him near you so that you can help him, is
as necessary to you as your food and drink. But there are people
enough who seem to thrive abundantly without one act of charity. No
self-sacrifice breaks the smooth level of their selfish days. They live

60

without that which is your very life. So of a multitude of things. To one man it is incredible that life can be worth having without wealth; another cannot understand how men can live without amusement; and another, with his social nature, looks at his friend who lives in solitude, and wonders how and why he lives at all.

But nowhere is all this so clear as in the matter of religion. One who is really living a religious life, one who is really trying to serve God, who is loving God and believes with all his heart that God loves him, who finds all through his daily life the thick-sown signs that he is not alone, that Christ is helping him and saving him, how strange and almost impossible it is for him to conceive of a life that has nothing of all that in it. How desolate it seems! How tame it looks! One man's days are full of "joy in the Holy Ghost." He is always looking up for inspiration and always receiving it. When he wants comfort there is the Comforter close beside him, nay, deep within him. And then he opens the gate into some brother's life and learns how he is living, and finds that there is nothing at all there of what is so dear to himself. That brother "has not so much as heard whether there be any Holy Ghost."

This was just the position in which St. Paul found himself at Ephesus. He had been a Christian now for many years. It was far back in the past, the time when Jesus had appeared to him at mid-day and made him His disciple. He had felt the powerful aid of the Holy Spirit in many a difficult moment of his life. All that he did and said was in the confidence and by the help of this unseen Friend who was nearer to him than any of his closest earthly friends. And now he came to Ephesus where there were some people who called themselves Christians, and looking for their sympathy and fellow-feeling he inquired, "Have ye received the Holy Ghost since ye believed?" And they said unto him, "We have not so much as heard if there be any Holy Ghost." What was everything to him, they knew nothing at all about. No wonder that his soul yearned over them and he stayed with them and taught them. We can picture his joy as gradually they became sharers in his happiness. What greater joy can any man desire than to bring any other man who has known nothing of it into the knowledge and the power of the Holy Ghost?

This is our subject for Whitsunday morning. What is it to know and not to know "whether there be any Holy Ghost"? Are there not many men among us who, if Paul asked them the old question, would have to give the old Ephesian answer? "Have you received the Holy Ghost, my friend?" Be honest, and must you not answer as they answered, "Indeed I have not so much as heard whether there be any Holy Ghost. The name indeed has sounded in my ears; but as a real person I have not got any true idea of His existence"? Indeed the element of personal experience is so involved with all our knowledge of the Holy Spirit, that for any man to say "Yes, I know Him," is a vastly profounder acknowledgment than the statement of any other knowledge. That is the reason why it is often so vague and hesitating; but just for the same reason there comes a time when a man certain of his experience can say "Yes, I have received, I do know the Holy Spirit" with a certainty and distinctness with which he cannot lay claim to the knowledge of any other thing or person.

In order to understand our question let us turn to this story of the Ephesians. They were Christian believers. They are called "disciples." They had been baptized after the baptism of John. They believed Christian truth and they accepted Christian duty. They had a knowledge of, a faith in Christ, but they had no knowledge of the Holy Spirit. The perception of a present God who should fill out belief in truth with personal apprehension, and who should make duty delightful by personal love, this they had not reached; no one had told them of it.

It was a strange condition. It is not easy to reconcile it with many of our Christian notions, but yet it is a condition which represents the state of many people whom we know, who seem to have just what they had and to be lacking in just what they wanted. I suppose a man — and it is not all a supposition, the specimens are all around us — who believes the Christian truths. That there is a God who made and governs everything, that this God has revealed Himself in Jesus Christ, that He has lived and taught among men, and that at last He died for men in all the torture of the cross, and rose out of the grave in all the inherent power of His immortality — this they believe. And all that God requires, all that Christ commanded, they accept. The duties of a good life, purity, honesty, resignation, self-denial, all of these they acknowledge. They try to do these duties. Their lives are often wonderful with the severe and lofty standards that they set themselves. They work heroically to fulfil the Master's will. Do we not know such men? They often puzzle us. The aim of all their life is high. Perhaps as I describe them you know that you are such a man yourself. You know that Christ is the great Master. His truth and His commandments you receive. But all the time you know that something is lacking — a vividness, a life, a spring, a hopefulness and courage which you hear of other people having, which you sometimes see suggested in the things you do, which you seem to be often just upon the verge of, but which after all you do not get, and for the lack of which you are forever conscious of a certain dryness in your belief and a certain shallowness in your duty. What is it that you lack? This lack which, if I speak to your consciousness at all, you recognize, this something which you want, I take to be precisely the Holy Spirit. I do not know any other way in which He can become so real to a true, earnest man, as in the realization of just this want.

Let us separate the two departments to which I have referred, and speak more particularly, first of Belief and then of Duty. We have all been familiar all our lives with the distinction between head-belief and heart-belief. We have been taught, sometimes in such a way that it puzzles us, sometimes in such a way that it was confirmed by all our deepest experience, that simply to know, even with the most unquestioning conviction, that certain things were true, was not really having faith in those things. We go up to the very limit of the belief that can come either by traditional acceptance or by the conviction which argument produces, and there we stand. We cannot advance one step farther. We seem to have exhausted all the power that is in us. But we are sure that out beyond there is a region which, though we cannot enter it, is real, and is the true completion of the region through which we have already travelled.

How familiar this is in our dealings with our friends! I meet a man whom I have heard of long. Every authority in which I trust has told me that that man is wise and good. I come to know him well, and for myself I see the evidence of his wisdom and goodness. He proves it to me by the things he does. I no more doubt it than I doubt the sun. I say that I believe in him and I do believe in him; but all the time I am aware that out beyond the limit of this belief which I have reached and on which I stand, there is a whole new country, the region of another sort of belief in him into which I have not entered, where if I could enter for an hour everything would be different and new. I may be helpless. I may not be able to drag my feet across the border. I may stand as if chained by magic on this line which separates the head's belief from the heart's confidence and trust; but, powerless as I may be to enter it, I know that all this other world is there, with the mists hanging over it and hiding it, but real and certain still, the land of personal friendship and communion.

And just the same is true of truths. I know that some great truth is true; our human immortality, let us say. Every one whom I trust has told me so. Those whose words are to me like gospel have assured me of it. I may even hear and believe that voice that speaks out of eternity itself. I may put full trust in the word of Christ which tells me that the dead are not dead but are living still. And my reason may be all convinced. I may be persuaded by every natural argument that the soul does not perish in its separation from the body, but goes on in its unbroken life. All this I steadfastly believe. But what then? Here I stand upon this clear sharp line. I am immortal. I say it over to myself and know that it is true. But still I am not satisfied. This certainty of immortality is nothing to me but a mere conviction. I get nothing out of it. It does not flow up into my duties and experiences. I am not stronger for it. I have not taken hold of it, nor has it taken hold of me. And, until this comes to pass, I feel a sense of incompleteness. I know in all my surest moments that there is an assurance which I have not reached. I know when my feet are planted the firmest on the outmost line of rational conviction that there is beyond that line a region of spiritual confidence which I have not entered.

Here then are the two kinds of belief in persons and in truths. What is the difference between them? The first is clear, definite, and strong. I know that he whom I believe in, be it man or God, is true and good. I know that the truth that I accept is certain and impregnable. But there is something hard, dry, literal, about my faith. I can write it all down and say all that I know about it in letters inscribed upon a book. I may contend for it vigorously, but I do not feed upon it. The other belief has in it just what this belief lacks. It has spirit. I cannot write it down in letters. My heart is full of it and it takes me right into the heart of the Being or the truth that I believe in.

Surely this difference is very clear. Surely we all know well enough that struggle after the heart and spirit of what our minds have accepted, which lets us understand it all. How often we have felt that disheartening certainty that we are holding tight the shells, the mere outside of our richest beliefs, and not getting at their soul and life. Sometimes have we not contended earnestly for our faith and told some unbeliever that he was losing precious truth because he did not hold it, and then gone off from our discussion saying to ourselves gloomily, "Yes, it is all true, but still, if he held it only on the outside as I do, would he be so much richer after all?" How often do we seem to ourselves to be like starving men, holding fruits that we know are rich and nutritious within, but cased in iron rinds which no pressure of ours is strong enough to break.

We are then very often where these Ephesians were. What came to them and saved them was the Holy Spirit. What must come to us and save us is the same Holy Spirit. There they were holding certain truths about God and Jesus, holding them drearily and coldly, with no life and spirit in their faith. Paul came to them and said, "These truths are true, but they are divine truths. You can really see them only as you are sharers in divinity yourself, and look at them with eyes enlightened by the intelligence of God. God must come into you and change you. His Spirit must come into you and occupy you; and then, looking with His Spirit, you shall see the spirit of the truths you look at; full of the Holy Ghost, the ghost, the heart, the soul of these great verities shall open itself in all its holiness to you. You shall see Jesus. You shall lay hold on immortality not on the outside but on the inside, in the very heart and spirit. Is not this intelligible, my dear friends? If Raphael could enter into you as you stand before his picture, would you not see deeper than you do now? Would not the Raphael in the picture come out from depths which you have never fathomed? If a child can be filled with the father's spirit, will not the spirit of the household, the intention, the purpose of it all, come out from the hard skeleton of its structure to meet the new spiritual apprehension? And so if you can be filled with God, will not the soul of God's truth of every sort, as you stand face to face with it, open to you deeper and deeper depths, changing your belief into a more and more profound and spiritual thing?

This was what Paul prayed for and this was what came to those Ephesians. God the Holy Spirit came into them and then their old belief opened into a different belief; then they really believed. Do you ask what we mean by that? Do you insist on knowing in exact statement how God entered into these people? Ah, if you ask that, you must ask in vain. If you insist upon not receiving God until you know how His life comes to your life, you must go on godless forever. You must know more than you do know, more than any man knows, of what man is and what God is and what are the mysterious channels that run from one life into the other, before you can tell how God flows into man and fills him with Himself. Tell me, if you can, the real nature of your friend's influence, the inflow of his life on yours that makes you full of him. Only one thing I think we can know about this filling of man by God, this communication of the Holy Spirit, that it is natural and not unnatural, that it is a restoral of communication, that it is a reenthronement of God where He belongs, that the prayer which invokes the Holy Ghost is the breaking down of an artificial barrier, and the letting in of the flood of divine life to flow where it belongs, in channels that were made for it. If we know this, then the occupation of man's life by God is simply a final fact. It is just like the occupation of the body by the soul. No man can tell how it is; but that it is, is testified by every form of human strength and beauty in which our eyes delight.

Pause then a moment and think what Whitsunday was, the first Whitsunday. We read the story of the miracle. We hear the rushing of the mighty wind and see the cloven tongues of fire quivering above the heads of the apostles. Perhaps we cannot understand it. It seems natural enough that when Jesus is born the sky should open and the angels sing; that when Jesus dies the skies should darken and the rocks should break. The great events were worthy of those miracles, or greater. But here at Pentecost what was there to call out such prodigies? If what we have said is true, was there not certainly enough? It was the coming back of God into man. It was the promise in these typical men of how near God would be to every man henceforth. It was the manifestation of the God Inspirer as distinct from and yet one with the God Creator and the God Redeemer. It was primarily the entrance of God into man and so, in consequence, the entrance of its spirit and full meaning into every truth that man could know. It was the blossom-day of humanity, full of the promise of unmeasured fruit.

And what that first Whitsunday was to all the world, one certain day becomes to any man, the day when the Holy Spirit comes to him. God enters into him and he sees all things with God's vision. Truths which were dead spring into life and are as real to him as they are to God. He is filled with the Spirit and straightway he believes; not as he used to, coldly holding the outsides of things. He has looked right into their hearts. His belief in Jesus is all afire with love. His belief in immortality is eager with anticipation. Can any day in all his life compare with that day? If it were to break forth into flames of fire and tremble with sudden and mysterious wind, would it seem strange to him — the day when he first knew how near God was, and how true truth was, and how deep Christ was? O have we known that day? O, careless, easy, cold believers! if one should come and ask you, "Have you received the Holy Ghost since you believed?" dare you, could you, answer him, "Yes"?

LET US take now a few moments to consider the other part of the Holy Spirit's influence, the way in which, when He enters into a soul, He not merely gives clearness to truth, but gives delight and enthusiastic impulse to duty. These Ephesians had not merely believed much Christian truth, they had been trying also to do what was right; they had accepted the Christian law so far as they knew it. We can think of them as very patient, persevering workers, struggling to do everything that they were told they ought to do. Now what did Paul do for them here when he brought them the knowledge of the Holy Spirit? I think the answer will be found in that verse of the Savior's in which He described what the Holy Spirit's work should be. "He shall take of mine and shall show it unto you," Jesus had said. The work of the Spirit was to make Jesus vividly real to men. What he did then for any poor Ephesian man or woman who was toiling away in obedience to the law of Christianity, was to make Christ real to the toiling soul behind and in the law. He took the laborer there in Ephesus who only knew that it was a law of Christianity that he ought to help his brethren, and made it as personal a thing, as really the wish of Christ that he should help his brethren, as it had been to the twelve disciples when they were living under Christ's eye, while he was with them in Judea or while they were distributing the bread and fish at his command to the hungry men by the sea of Galilee. This was the change which the Holy Spirit made in Duty. He filled it with Christ, so that every laborer had the strength, the courage, the incitement to fidelity which comes from working for one whom the worker knows and loves.

And very often when our tasks are pressing on us is not this the change we need? Your Christian duties, the prayers you pray, the self-denials that you practise, the charities you give — what is the matter with them? The temptations you resist, the good word that you speak to some brother, the way you teach your class, the way you condemn some prevailing sin — what is the matter with them all? What is the reason why they are so dull and tame? Why are they not strong enthusiastic work? The reason must be that there is no clear person for whom you do these things. You serve yourself, and how clear you are to yourself; and so, what life there is in every act of your own service; but you serve Christ and how dim He has grown! and so, how listlessly the hands move at His labor! Now if the Holy Spirit can indeed bring Him clearly to you, is not the Holy Spirit what you need? And this is just exactly what He does. I find a Christian who has really "received the Holy Ghost," and what is it that strikes and delights me in him? It is the intense and intimate reality of Christ. Christ is evidently to him the clearest person in the universe. He talks to Christ. He dreads to offend Christ. He delights to please Christ. His whole life is light and elastic with this buoyant desire of doing everything for Jesus, just as Jesus would wish it done. So simple, but so powerful! So childlike, but so heroic! Duty has been transfigured. The weariness, the drudgery, the whole task-nature, has been taken away. Love has poured like a new life-blood along the dry veins, and the soul that used to toil and groan and struggle goes now singing along its way, "The life that I now live in the flesh, I live by the faith of the Son of God who loved me and gave Himself for me."

O my dear friends, have you received the Holy Ghost since you believed? Since you began to do your duty has any revelation come to you of Him who is the Lord of duty? Have you caught any sight of Christ, and begun to know what it is to do it all for Him? Has the love with which He lived and died for you been so brought home to you that you are longing only to thank Him by a grateful and obedient life? Have you so made Him yours that He has made you His? If so, the life of heaven has begun for you. Only to know Him more and more forever and so to grow into completer and completer service, there is your eternity already marked out before you. It stretches out and is lost beyond where you can see; but it all stretches in the one direction in which your face is set; deepening knowledge, bringing deeper love, forever opening into more and more faithful service. Go on into the richest developments of that life, led by the power of the Holy Ghost.

BOTH IN belief and in duty then, this is the work of the Holy Spirit: to make belief profound by showing us the hearts of the things that we believe in; and to make duty delightful by setting us to doing it for Christ. O, in this world of shallow believers and weary, dreary workers, how we need that Holy Spirit! Remember, we may go our way, ignoring all the time the very forces that we need to help us do our work. The forces still may help us. The Holy Spirit may help us, will surely help us, just as far as He can, even if we do not know His name or ever call upon Him. But there is so much more that He might do for us if we would only open our hearts and ask Him to come into them. Remember, He is God, and God is love. And no man ever asks God to come into his heart and holds his heart open to God, without God's entering. Children, on this Whitsunday pray the dear God, the blessed Holy Spirit, to come and live in your heart and show you Jesus, and make you love to do what is right for His sake. Old men, aspire to taste already here what is to be the life and joy of your eternity. Men and women in the thick of life, do not go helpless when there is such help at hand; do not go on by yourselves, struggling for truth and toiling at your work, when the Holy Spirit is waiting to show you Christ, and to give you in Him the profoundness of faith and the delightfulness of duty.

Let us come to Christ's Communion Table and celebrate our union with Him and with one another, putting all fear and selfishness aside, and praying Him to show us there how rich a thing it is to believe in Him and how sweet a thing it is to serve Him by His Holy Spirit.

# The Consolations of God

*Are the consolations of God small with thee?*

Job xv.11

I f we could fully tell each other our thoughts of God, or if we could look with perfect clearness into one another's hearts, and see what thought of the great Father is lying there, no doubt the variety of our conceptions of Him would surprise us very much. He must appear so differently to His different children; and while this difference of our ideas of God indicates, no doubt, in part our blindness and half-sightedness, it indicates still more the many-sidedness of His great nature. He has a different side of Himself to show to each of us.

But this is not all. Not only to different men does God give different impressions of Himself, but on different parts of the same man's life He shines with very different lights and colors. Can we remember when we were children, and had our own thoughts of God, how very strange, how hard to grasp appeared the pictures of Him which seemed to give our elders such delight; the accounts which we read in grown-up people's books, or heard in the sermons of grown-up ministers? The truly live and growing Christian might mark the different stages of his advancing life by the different aspects which he saw of God. He might recognize his fifteenth year by one sort of revelation of the Fatherhood, and his twenty-fifth by another, and his fiftieth by another. It would be a noble biography — the history of the sun's rising, and of the different stories that it told of itself, the different shadows that it cast, until its perfect noon. It may be that in eternity there shall be some such ageless condition as shall comprise the vision of all ages, and take in at once the whole character of God; but here the beauty of living lies largely in the way in which we are always coming in sight of new characteristics and capacities in Him.

I want to speak today about God as the Consoler. "Are the consolations of God small with thee?" And I have been led to these opening words by thinking how this side of God's life shows itself only to certain conditions of this life of ours. It is not for everybody. It is not for the very young and joyous. You would not go to a young man just bursting through the open doors of life, radiant with health, eager for work, with an infinite sense of vitality, and say, "Come, here is God, who consoles men. Give yourself to Him." To such a soul you have something else to say: "Here is God the Strengthener. Here is the Setter of great tasks; the God who holds His crown of victory on the tops of high mountains up which His eager-hearted young heroes may climb to win it; the God who asks great sacrifices and who gives glorious rewards." That is what you would say, or what you ought to say, to the young strong man to whom you want to make God known. You say nothing about the God of repair, the God of consolation, the God who takes the broken life into His hands and mends it; nothing of that God yet. The time will come for that. And is there anything more touching and pathetic in the history of man than to see how absolutely, without exception, the men and women who start out with only the need of tasks, of duties, of something which can call out their powers, and of the smile of God stimulating and encouraging them — how they all come, one by one, certainly up to the place in life where they need consolation? I will tell you what it seems to me like. Have you ever seen, or perhaps made one of, a party of people who were going to explore some deep, dark cavern — the Mammoth Cave of Kentucky, or the Catacombs of Rome? They all stand out in the sunlight, and the attendants, who know the journey they are going to make, pass round among them and put into the hands of each a lighted candle. How useless it seems. How pale and colorless the little flame appears in the gorgeous flood of sunlight. But the procession moves along. One after another enters the dark cavern's mouth. One after another loses the splendor of day-light. In the hands of one after another the feeble candle-flame comes out bright in the darkness, and by and by they are all walking in the dark, holding fast their candles as if they were their very life; totally dependent now upon what seemed so useless half an hour ago. That seems to me to be a picture of the way in which God's promises of consolation, which we attach but very little meaning to at first, come out into beauty and value as we pass on into our lives. The nature begins to break somewhere. Perhaps the physical strength gives way first. Long before the courage of the heart or the mind's quick activity is dimmed, the knees refuse their office and the heart beats slow. It is an epoch in a man's life when he takes his first medicine to repair the ravages of time, the wear of the machine. Before he has taken food for support; now he takes medicine for repair. He has reached his need of consolation. Or perhaps it is the spirit that gives way before the body breaks. No matter in what order the new need arrives, there is something pathetic in the way in which it comes to everybody. The social life decays, or with one dreadful blow is dashed to pieces. The perfect trust we had in one another is dislodged. The courage goes out on its task and brings back no booty of success. The terrible disappointment in self, the conscious-ness of sin, bursts or creeps in upon us, and then the hands for the first time are reached out for consolation, and the great doors — which we have hardly noticed as we passed and repassed on this side of the Divine nature, they were shut so close, and we saw so little need of enter-ing this way — are flung, wide open to take the tired and disappointed creature in. It is as if we had sailed gayly all day up and down a glorious coast, rejoicing in the winds that swept around its headlands and caught our sails, thinking the bolder the coast the better, never asking whether there were a place of refuge anywhere; till at last the storm burst upon us, and then we never thought the coast so beautiful as when we saw her open an unexpected harbor, and take us into still wa-ter behind the rocks that we had been glorying in, out of the tempest's reach.

The world seems to have lived the same life, with the same succes-sion of experiences in which each man lives. What is the old story of the book of Genesis but this — the tale of how the world came to need, and, when it needed, found God the consoler? There was no talk of consolation in those walks beneath the trees, before the sin, when man and his Maker held mysterious converse in ways which we with our blinded senses cannot know. How many ages slipped by so, who can tell? But by and by the catastrophe whose fruits are in all men's lives came, and now instantly a new power in God was touched. In all the anger of God in these first chapters of the Book of Life after the fall, we feel still that we have touched a before unmanifested power of His nature. With the first promise of repair, the first suggestion of a Redeemer, He has opened His power of consolation. It is as if we saw a father stoop, and for the first time pick up and set upon his feet the child who thus far had run strongly on and needed only to be guided. It gives us a new sight into the heart of his fatherhood; and so since Eden the world has rested, not merely on the helps and the commandments, but on the consolations of God.

When we think about the death of children, and of the other life on which they enter after they have left this world, it seems as if it must be an everlasting difference in that life for them, that they have never known what it is to be consoled by God. That they will be less happy, no man can say; for who shall compare with one another the perfect happinesses of Heaven? But surely there must be something of God that has been shown to His venerable servant, who has been consoled a thousand times, whose life has been broken again and again, and again and again repaired by God; something that he knows of God which never can be known to the little child whose life, from its first beginning here to the very end of its eternity, never sinned or sorrowed, and so never needed repair or consolation.

And yet we cannot say how early in this life of ours the God of consolation may be needed, and may show Himself to the needy soul. I would not seem to count out of my subject for today those of my people, the youngest, the happiest, the most hopeful, on whom I should be sorry any Sunday to turn my back and say, "There is nothing for you today." Perhaps their hearts will tell me that they have sorrows and disappointments of their own. And certainly they have, and it is the glory of God's consolations that they reach every grade and kind of need. The child with his sorrows has as much right to them as the man with his. Indeed, there is one view in which no trouble of man is great enough, and then there is another view in which no trouble of man is too small, to be worthy of touching the heart of God. And so let us count nobody out; let us all come together and try to find what God's consolations are; try to find how God consoles His people.

1. What I shall say will be good for nothing, will be mere theorizing, unless I simply draw out our own experience of God into description, and tell how He really has consoled us all. Let me say, then, first of all, that God is the consoler of man by the very fact of His existence. There is a class of passages in the Bible which to me seem mysteriously beautiful, and which appear to rest the peace of the human soul upon the mere fact of the existence of the larger life of God. Such is that verse of the forty-sixth Psalm, "Be still, and know that I am God." "Thou shalt know that I, the Lord, am," is the noble promise that comes again and again, full of reassurance. And when God's people, trampled, bruised, broken, trodden in the dust in Egypt, asked by Moses for the name of the God who had promised them His deliverance, it was a mere assertion of the awful and supreme existence that was given in reply: "I AM hath sent me." No doubt in all such cases there is active character within the mere existence and coming out clearly through it, and this character has its declared relations to the man who needs consoling, but still it is primarily the fact of existence. It is because God is that man is bidden to be at peace. And this is not hard to understand. If anybody has ever felt that his life, with its little woes, was easier to bear because there were great men living the same human life with him, he can understand it perfectly. The men of larger life of whom he knew never came near him, never touched his life, never spoke to him, perhaps never knew of his existence. It may be they were merely men whose lives he had read in books. For here is one of the greatest uses of really great history and biography, in their peace-giving and consoling power. It was not what the great men of the world had done. It was simply that they had existed. I pity the man who has never in his best moods felt his life consoled and comforted in its littleness by the larger lives that he could look at and know that they too were men, living in the same humanity with himself, only living in it so much more largely.

For so much of our need of consolation comes just in this way, from the littleness of our life, its pettiness and weariness insensibly transferring itself to all life, and making us skeptical about anything great or worth living for in life at all; and it is our rescue from this debilitating doubt that is the blessing which falls upon us when, leaving our own insignificance behind, we let our hearts rest with comfort on the mere fact that there are men of great, broad, generous, and healthy lives — men like the greatest that we know.

Indeed the power of mere activity is often overrated. It is not what the best men do, but what they are, that constitutes their truest benefaction to their fellow-men. The things that men do get their chief value, after all, from the way in which they are able to show the existence of character which can comfort and help mankind. Certainly, in our own little sphere, it is not the most active people to whom we owe the most. Among the common people whom we know it is not necessarily those who are busiest, not those who, meteor-like, are ever on the rush after some visible change and work. It is the lives, like the stars, which simply pour down on us the calm light of their bright and faithful being, up to which we look and out of which we gather the deepest calm and courage. It seems to me that there is reassurance here for many of us who seem to have no chance for active usefulness. We can do nothing for our fellow-men. But still it is good to know that we can be something for them; to know (and this we may know surely) that no man or woman of the humblest sort can really be strong, gentle, pure, and good, without the world being better for it, without somebody being helped and comforted by the very existence of that goodness.

And now just so it is with God's life and the life of man. Here is an atheist. He is a thoughtful, conscientious man, but by failure after failure his life has been broken down into a low and hopeless tone. He has come to a terrible doubt whether there is any such thing as being good. He seems a mere sham to himself, and all his fellow-men are shams around him. Give what account he will of what men call righteousness, he has really lost the belief of absolute morality altogether. He is demoralized. He has fallen down into the wretched theories of expediency, and he hates himself for lying there, and yet he cannot get away. Does not that man need consolation? Poor fellow, with his broken wings and bewildered brain, where is the man that has any such need as he has to be taken up into some strong, wise arms, and to be refreshed, repaired, remoralized? And then suddenly or gradually it is made known to this man that there is a perfect God. Is that nothing to him? The God does not speak to him yet. He does not know that the God cares for him; not even that the God is aware of him. Only this, that the God is; that purity is not a delusion, and justice not a guess, for there is a perfectly pure, just Being; there is a righteous one. Is it not like the sunrising to that poor broken man? Is he not comforted? I do not believe that there is any darkest, deepest dungeon under any horrible old castle, most utterly and hopelessly out of the reach of sunlight, in which it would not bring a new pang to the heart of the poor wretch imprisoned there if he knew that the sun, which he never saw and never should see again, was gone out of the heavens. Although he lives utterly in the dark, the knowledge that there is sunlight helps him and he is not quite desperate. Although we live petty and foolish lives, the knowledge that there is greatness and wisdom, the knowledge that there is God, is a far greater and more constant consolation to us than we know.

2. But we must go a great deal further than this. We begin with the knowledge of God's existence, and that consoles us when we are in perplexity and sorrow. Many and many a heart has entered into that knowledge, and found it the entrance into peace. But what comes next? The sympathy of this same God whose existence is already real to us. It becomes known to us not merely that He is, but that He cares for us. Not merely His life, but His love, becomes a fact. Surely this is a great step forward. We had to convince ourselves perhaps that there was not something cold and distant in the thought of the divine existence as a source of human consolation. We know that that thought does wonderfully help those to whom it is very real, but it is not so easy to understand beforehand that it will help men to know of the great "I AM." But here there can be no doubt. Any one will say, "If I could only be sure that He, the God of all things, really cares for me; that when any sorrow comes to me, it strikes right at His heart, and He is sorry too — if I could be sure of this, I do not know of anything I could not bear. What is there that I could not tolerate? Nay, what is there that I would not almost welcome, if it could by any violence break open a way by which

God could come down to me and show me that perfect nature as my friend, my helper, thoughtful for my welfare and my woe?" Nor is this all mere selfishness. I rather like to think that the real reason why the sufferer rejoices in the sympathy of God is that thereby, through love, that dear and perfect nature after which he has struggled before is made completely known to him. Love is the translating medium. It is not merely that now that whose absolute existence he had comprehended already has become his; that he is reaping the benefit of that which before he had regarded only as absolutely being. It is not only that the sky, which hung in majesty and peace over the whole earth, at last has dropped its rain upon his garden. It is rather that through this special love for him, the absolute and everlasting Deity has been made known to him. It is that through God's sympathy he knows God more intensely and more nearly, and so all the consolations of God's being have become more real to him.

I think that this is so. I think that any sensitive and thoughtful soul will feel the real distinction. And yet I do not think much of such distinctions. I know we do not gain, but rather lose, by any attempt to separate the elements of comfort that come to man's soul in the one complete round gift of the sympathy of God. Who shall attempt to describe the indescribable, and tell the power of sympathy? You go to see your friend on whom some great sorrow has fallen. You sit beside him. You look into his eyes. You say a few broken and faltering words. And then you go away disheartened. How entirely you have failed to do for him that which you went to do, that which you would have given the world to do. How you have seemed only to intrude on him with vulgar curiosity when you really longed to help him. How many times you have done this, and then how many times you have been afterwards surprised to find that you really did help him with that silent visit. My dear friends, never let the seeming worthlessness of sympathy make you keep back that sympathy of which, when men are suffering around you, your heart is full. Go and give it without asking yourself whether it is worth the while to give it. It is too sacred a thing for you to tell what it is worth. God, from whom it comes, sends it through you to His needy child. Do not ever let any low skepticism make you distrust it, but speak out what God has put it in your heart to speak to any sufferer. The sympathy of God for man has just this same difficulty about it, if we try to analyze it. We cannot say that He has done anything for us. We cannot tell even of any thought that He has put into our minds. Merely He has been near us. He has known that we were in trouble and He has been sorry for us.

How do we learn of such a sympathy of God? How can we really come to believe that He knows our individual troubles, and sorrows for them with us? I think that this is a hard question for a great many people. The magnitude of the world, the multitudes of souls that God has made, perplexes many hearts, and makes it very hard for them to believe in personal, individual sympathy and care. More than from any abstract or scientific arguments about the universality of great laws, I think it is the bigness of the world, the millions upon millions of needy souls, that makes it hard for men to believe in the discriminating care and personal love of God for each. Our wider view across the world, the readiness with which we take in all the millions of our fellow-men, makes it harder for us. The Jew, shut up in his little nation, found it easier. In such perplexity what shall we do? I know only the most simple answers. In the first place, give free and bold play to those instincts of the heart which believe that the Creator must care for the creatures He has made, and that the only real effective care for them must be that which takes each of them into His love, and knowing it separately surrounds it with His separate sympathy. In the next place, open the heart to that same conviction as it has been profoundly pressed upon the hearts of multitudes of men everywhere. It is not inconceivable. It is only the special prominence of certain ideas in our time which have made some people think it inconceivable that a personal God should care separately for every one of His million children. It is not inconceivable when such multitudes of men have conceived it, have rested their whole weight upon that assurance, have run into the shelter of that certainty whenever the storm was too high and too strong for them. Above all, get the great spirit of the Bible. Read into the heart of the Book of Life until you are thoroughly possessed with its idea — the idea which gives it its whole consistency and shape, the idea without which it would all drop to pieces — that there is not one life which the Life Giver ever loses out of His sight; not one which sins so that He casts it away; not one which is not so near to Him that whatever touches it touches Him with sorrow or with joy. I know nothing which can secure a man from the sad skepticism about the personal sympathy of God, like a complete entrance into the atmosphere and spirit of the Bible, in which that sympathy is the first accepted fact of life.

3. By His existence and by His felt sympathy, then, God gives His consolations to the souls of those who need them. But more than this. When your friend is in trouble you first of all try to remind him, in some most unobtrusive way, that you are living and that you are his friend. Any little token of your life, a gift of flowers, or any trifle, will do that. Then you go and sit down by him, and without a word let him know not merely in general that you are his friend, but that you are very sorry for him in this special sorrow. But if you really respect him and care for his whole nature, you want to do something more than that. You want, in the kindest and gentlest way, to get certain great consoling thoughts home to his bruised and broken heart. You are not satisfied until the reason, too, has found its consolation, and through its open doors comfort has spread through the part of his nature which is open to that access. And so it is with God. He, too, has His great truths, His ideas which He brings to the hearts He wishes to console. He does not treat His sufferers like children who are simply to be petted with soft words, and patted with soft hands till they forget their grief. He deals with them as men who are capable of knowing the meanings, the explanations, and the purposes of the troubles that come to them. And so He gives them His great truths of consolation. What are those truths? Education, spirituality, and immortality — these seem to be the sum of them. You are in great distress. Your friend is gone. Your life is broken. Your soul is stunned. Is it possible that, sitting still or walking drearily about in your grief, God should make you know education or the law of growth, the endless principle of the sacrifice of a present for a better future; should reveal spirituality, and make you know the soul's value as far superior to anything that can concern the outer life; should open to you immortality, and show you the endlessness of His plans, so that what has seemed to your wretchedness to be complete and finished, should appear to be only just begun, and not ready to be judged of yet? Is there no consolation in these great thoughts? They do

not take your sorrow off; and oh, my dear friend, whatever be your suffering, I beg you to learn first of all that not that, not to take your sorrow off, is what God means, but to put strength into you that you may carry it as the tired man, who has drunk the strength-giving river, lifts up his burden by the river-bank and goes singing on his way. Be sure your sorrow is not giving you its best unless it makes you a more thoughtful man than you have ever been before, unless it opens to you ideas that have before been unfamiliar; mostly these three ideas, education, spirituality, immortality. Those ideas are the keys of all the mysteries of life, and so the gateways to consolation. And it is wonderful to see how, just as soon as a man is really crushed and sorrowful, God seems by every avenue to be offering those great ideas for that man's acceptance. He seems to write them on the sky, to whisper them from every movement of the commonest machinery of life, to fill books with them that never seemed to know anything of them before, to make the vacant house and the full grave declare them. You are a child of God whom He is training. You have a soul which is your true value. You are to live forever. Know these truths. By them triumph over the sorrow that He cannot take away, and be consoled.

4. But even this is not all. God consoles us by what He is, by what He feels for us, by what He teaches us. But all these, as I tell them over, seem to have something passive about them. They show God sitting as it were, and letting His life flow out in blessing upon the emptied life that needs Him. But there is hardly a sufferer who does not crave something more active, if we may say so. He wants to feel, at any rate he thinks how blessed it would be if he could feel, God doing something on his life, showing his sympathy by some strong act. "Bow thy heavens, O Lord, and come down," he cries; "touch the mountains and they shall smoke." And so he prays for God to help him, to do something positive for him. What shall it be? Men are puzzled a good deal about prayer nowadays. I suppose a good many men have really stopped praying for some things which they used to pray for, and for some things which God very much wishes them to pray for still. But the prayer of men for what their souls will always count the greatest miracle of God, for spiritual regeneration, for newer, deeper, holier lives, that prayer has probably not been much affected by all the speculations about prayer.

It is prayed just as often and as earnestly as ever, and so it will continue to be as long as men's souls continue to bear witness to the power and reality with which it is answered. "Create in me a clean heart, O God, and renew the right spirit within me." Men will keep on praying that so long as they believe there is a God, even if they have long ceased to pray for the changing of the wind and the stopping of the pestilence. And so when a man in trouble prays God to do something for him, this is the real miracle by which God stands ready to answer that man's prayer. He will not send an angel as He did to the women at the tomb, but He will come Himself and show His presence and His power by working the miracle of regeneration upon the soul that has cried out for Him. My dear friends, that is the consummate consolation; everything leads up to that. I see a poor creature sitting in sorrow. He catches sight of God's existence and he is helped. God sends him assurance of His sympathy, and a smile finds its way across the face that seemed all given up to sorrow, and looked as if it would never smile again. God teaches him His truth, and the disheartened heart remembers once more what it was to be brave and strong. But then God comes and takes that soul, and positively, strongly lifts it up and away into the new life. He forgives the man for his sin, and He gives him the new heart. He lays the same strong hand on him that Christ laid upon the leper. He speaks the same sweet word to him that Christ spoke to the adulteress. He forgives him and converts him. He makes him a new man; and then, when the man stands up new, no longer crushed by his sorrow, and yet certainly, thank God, certainly, not having passed out of his sorrow! — but made a new man by the touch of God through his sorrow, to him, standing there with his new life before him, a new peace in his face, a new courage in his arm, a new love in his heart — come to himself as the new man comes by the sacrifice of himself, come to himself by having come to God — when we look into his glowing face, and ask the old question that Eliphaz asked of Job, "Are the consolations of God small with thee?" how quick and sure his answer comes back: "No, very great!" Nay, he is able to take these great words of David which it is so terrible to hear people use when they do not mean them, and he fills them with meaning, as he says with serious joy, "It is good for me that I have been afflicted."

81

Are the consolations of God small with thee? His existence, His sympathy, His truth, His power. As I recount them all, it seems to me so great and beautiful to be the child of such a God. And pain and suffering grow holy when we think how through them the Father comes to His children. Let us not be cheated by mere theories to say that sorrow is not dreadful. Let us not stand here in perfect health with our unbroken friendships and dare to say that sickness is not wearisome, and bereavement is not sad. We only mock the sufferers all round us when we say that. It is very cruel. But let us claim that if a man really is close to God there is a victory over the pain and a transfiguration of the sadness. "If a man is close to God." Can we say that and not remember how the Godhood and the manhood met in the Incarnation? Can we say that and not remember that all we have been saying was supremely realized when the Son of God was born and lived and died for us? God's being! Who could doubt it, as He walked the streets, and men saw God in His face? He brought it with Him across the threshold of the temple, and through the low doorway of the cottage of Bethany. God's pity! Who did not see it as He laid His hands upon the children's heads and looked down, from the Mount of Olives, on Jerusalem? God's truth! Who must not hear it speaking as He talks with Nicodemus, or preaches from the mountain? God's power! What more has it any need of proof, when the finger laid upon the hem of His garment gives the lost health back again, when the death upon the cross is the salvation of the world? All that there is consolatory in God — being, sympathy, truth, power — Christ has set in the clearness and the splendor of His life.

And so if you want consolation you must come to Him. It is not a dead phrase. It was not dead when He spoke it first in Jerusalem, and said "Come to me." It was the very word of life. You must come to Him, know Him, love Him, serve Him. In His church and His service you must take your place. Nay, let us not say "must." Our duties are always best stated as our privileges. You may come to Him, for He has said, "Come unto me all ye that are weary and heavy laden, and I will give you rest." May we all come nearer and nearer to Him always, and find peace.

# The Need of Self-Respect

—ᴍ—

*And He said unto me: Son of man, stand upon thy feet, and I will speak unto thee.*

Ezekiel ii.1

There are many passages in the Bible which describe the servants of God, as their Lord's messages came to them, falling upon their faces on the earth, and in that attitude of most profound humiliation listening to what God had to say. Moses, Joshua, David, Daniel, they are all seen at one time or another prostrate, and signifying their readiness to receive what God should tell them by the complete disowning of anything like worth or dignity in themselves. There is a great truth set forth in all such pictures. It is that only to human humility can God speak intelligibly. Only when a man is humble can he hear and understand the words of God. But in the passage which I have taken for my text this morning, there is another picture with another truth. When God was going to give a message to Ezekiel, He said to him, "Son of man, stand upon thy feet, and I will speak unto thee." Not on his face but on his feet; not in the attitude of humiliation but in the attitude of self-respect; not stripped of all strength, and lying like a dead man waiting for life to be given him, but strong in the intelligent consciousness of privilege, and standing alive, ready to cooperate with the living God who spoke to him; so the man now is to receive the word of God. I hope that we shall be able to comprehend this idea largely and truly

83

enough to see that it is not contradictory to the other, but certainly it is different from it. When God raised Ezekiel and set him on his feet before He spoke to him, was it not a declaration of the truth that man might lose the words of God because of a low and grovelling estimate of himself, as well as because of a conceited one? The best understanding of God could come to man only when man was upright and self-reverent in his privilege as the child of God.

If this be true, is it not a great truth? Is it not a truth well worthy of being set out in one of these graphic Bible-pictures, and one that needs continually to be preached? The other truth is often urged upon us; that if we are proud we shall be ignorant; if we do not listen humbly we shall listen in vain to hear the Divine voice of which the world is full. We are pointed continually to men on every side who have evidently no wisdom but their own, because they have never deeply felt that they needed any other, and who, therefore, are filling the land with their foolishness. But this other truth is not so often preached, nor, I think, so generally felt; unless you honor your life you cannot get God's best and fullest wisdom; unless you stand upon your feet you will not hear God speak to you.

There is much today of thoughtless and foolish depreciation of man and his condition. I want upon Thanksgiving Day, in the light of the Thanksgiving truth, to enter a quiet, earnest and profoundly sincere protest against it. I want to claim that it is blind to facts. I want to assert that it is not truly humble. I want to denounce it as the very spirit of ignorance, shutting men's ears hopelessly against the hearing of all the highest truth. The question comes to us most pressingly today. Shall we, can we, thank God for His mercies, standing upon our feet and rejoicing that we are men, thoroughly grateful for the real joy of life? Back of all the special causes for thanksgiving which our hearts recognize, is there a thankfulness for that on which they all rest and in which they are sewn like jewels in a cloth of gold; for the mere fact of human life, for the mere privilege and honor of being men and women? If there is not this, no gratitude is possible; or only such a gratitude as the poor wretch in his dungeon, for whom life has been robbed of every charm, feels to his jailor who thrusts through the window to him the crust of bread and jug of water which are to prolong his miserable life.

It may seem like an awful and unreasonable question; but indeed it is not so. The latest, and in many quarters the favorite, philosophy of the day — that which boasts itself as being the supreme achievement of the nineteenth century, the perfect flower of the wisdom of mankind — is that which under its fantastic name of Pessimism, declares deliberately that human life is a woe and a curse, and that the "will to live" is the fiend which persecutes humanity, which must be utterly destroyed before man can be happy. So speaks philosophy; and when we talk with unphilosophical men who have no theory, I think we are astonished to see how their view of life is essentially what this philosophy would give them. Either in the soft way or the hard way, either in sentimental whimperings or in dogged, rude defiance, men are saying that life is miserable. Either in large or little view, either looking at the great course of history or at the petty course of their own lives, men say the world is growing worse from day to day. The calm pessimism of the schools becomes the querulous discontent of the street philosopher, or the bitter cynicism of the newspaper satirist, or, what is far more significant than either, the silent distress and bewilderment of the man who sees no bright hope for himself or fellow-man. I am sure you know whereof I speak. In large circles of life (and they are just those circles in which a great many of us live) there is an habitual disparagement of human life, its joys and its prospects. Man is on his face. It seems to me that he must hear God's voice calling him to another attitude, or he is hopeless. "Son of man, stand upon thy feet, and I will speak unto thee."

What shall we say then of this prevalent depression as to the character and hopes of our human life, which is, I think, one of the symptoms of our time? Sometimes it is very sweeping and talks despairingly of man in general. Sometimes it is special and merely believes that our own age or our own land is given up to moral corruption and decay. As to its general character, I think it may be said that it comes from an inspection of human life which is neither the shallowest nor the deepest. It has got below the surface facts and first appearances of things, but it has not got down to their essential and central truth. The surface of the earth is warm with the direct rays of the sun. The center of the earth, perhaps, is warm with its own essential and quenchless fire. But between the two, after you get below the warm surface, and before you approach the warm heart of the globe, it is all cold and damp and dark and dreary. And so there is the surface sight of life, which is bright and enthusiastic. There is the sight of life which is deeper than this, which is sad and puzzled. There is the deepest sight of all, which is bright again with a truer light, and enthusiastic again with a soberer but a more genuine happiness. The character of the first sight, the most simple and superficial, very few people will be inclined to dispute. There are not many misanthropes who will deny that the first aspect of things which meets the eye of man is tempting and exhilarating. The external world is too manifestly beautiful; the sun is too bright, the fields too green, the sea too blue, the breeze too fresh, the luxuries of taste and sound and smell too manifold and sweet; the human frame is strung too thickly with the faculties of pleasure; the first and universal relationships of men, friendship and childhood and fatherhood, are too spontaneous sources of delight for any reasonable man to say that the first and simplest aspect of human life is not a happy thing. The charm may be only apparent, but at least there is an apparent charm. These men may be very foolish to find such joy in life, but certainly the men whom we see do find joy in it. To the child it is all joyous. Sometimes the right foot breaks through the thin crust for a moment, but the spring of the young walker sets him the next instant on the crust again, with only sufficient sense of danger to exhilarate, not to depress. And many men who never cease to be children keep the first sight of life all through, and never see below its bright surface nor hear another sound behind the music of its most palpable delights. So that the first aspect of life makes the bright optimist which every live and healthy boy ought to be and is. But this is only on the surface, as most men soon find out. It is real but superficial. By and by the exceptions and the contradictions and the limitations begin to show themselves. This first happiness of life is spotted with unhappiness; and it is not enough, even if it were unspotted, to satisfy the man who tries to find his satisfaction in it. Then comes the danger of misanthropy. There, just below the surface, lie the abject or defiant misanthropes; the men who count the sick people till they say there is no health, who count the dull days till they say there is no sunshine, who count the failures till they say there is no success, who count the frauds till they declare there is no honesty, and the fools till they laugh at the idea of wisdom. You see they have crawled down out of the sunlight. They have left the surface and its simple presumptions to burrow just under them among the exceptions and contradictions. They keep the same idea of what the purpose of life is and what sort of happiness it ought to have; only, while the boy in his optimism cried, as he saw the bird flash up in the sunlight, "Here it is," the middle-aged pessimist creeps with the mole underground and says, "It is not anywhere." Now what comes deeper still? What is there more profound than the lamentations over the sin and misery of life, which have succeeded to the first enthusiastic praise of everything, which came first of all? What is the next step if a man can take it? I answer, certainly a new idea of what life is for, of what happiness a man really needs; that is what must come. The notion of education and of character as the end of life, of something which a man is to be made, and by the power to make which all of life's experiences are to be judged, that opens to a man; and as he passes into that he finds the heat beginning to glow once more around him. He is coming in to the warm center of the world. There come forth adaptations for the higher work in things which have seemed wholly unfitted to produce the lower. Things which never could have made a man happy, develop a power to make him strong. Strength and not happiness, or rather only that happiness which comes by strength, is recognized as the end of human living. And with that test and standard the lost order and beauty reappear. The world is man's servant and friend; and man, full of the deeper self-respect, is ready to hear deeper and diviner messages of God.

This is the order. This is the way in which we pass to deeper knowledge, which is always tending to the happiest knowledge of our own life. First, life is a success because the skies are bright and the whole world is beautiful. Then life is a failure, because every joy is in danger of disappointment, and every confidence may prove untrue. Then life is a success again because through disappointment and deceit it still has power to make a man pure and strong. He who has delighted in the outside pleasures and then bowed down in misery because they disappeared, rises up at last and stands upon his feet when he discovers that God has a far deeper purpose about him than to keep him gay and cheerful, and that is to make him good; and with that deepest intention no accidents can interfere; with that discovery all his despair disappears, and a self-respect, which is full of hope and ready for intelligence, comes in its place.

This is the way in which a man's despair or contempt about himself is thoroughly undermined, by his getting a truer view of what the world and all its treatments of man's life are for. But now, I think, another fact comes in. Many men own the possibility of good which is open to them, while still they are despairing or cynical about the world itself, about the course of human life in general. There are many good people, I believe, who devoutly recognize the chance of character, of spiritual culture, which is offered to them by living in the midst of a world of sin and sorrow; but the sinful and sorrowful world itself seems to them desperate. They may be purified, but the fire that purifies them is the burning up of a miserable world. This is the strange hopelessness about the world, joined to a strong hope for themselves, which we see in many good religious people. It is what really lies at the heart of all the exclusive and seemingly selfish systems of religion, what makes it possible for good men to believe in election. In their own hearts they recognize indubitably that God is saving them, while the aspect of the world around them seems to show them that the world is going to perdition. That is a common enough condition of mind; but I think it may be surely said that it is not a good, nor can it be a permanent, condition. God has mercifully made us so that no man can constantly and purely believe in any great privilege for himself unless he believes in at least the possibility of the same privilege for other men. A man's hold on his own privilege either disappears or grows impure the moment that he gives the rest of the world up in despair. Under this principle, no man who believes that the world at large is growing hopelessly worse, can keep a lively and effectual hope that he himself is growing better. Indeed this is the danger of that current habit of depreciating man, and especially of depreciating our own times and surroundings, which is very common among us. It is not merely a speculative opinion. It is an influence which must reach a man's character. A man can have no high respect for himself unless he has a high respect for his human kind. He can have no strong hope for himself unless he has a strong hope for his human kind. And so, whatever be his pure tastes and lofty principles, one trembles for any man whom he hears hopelessly decrying human life in general, or the special condition of his own time.

It is time, perhaps, that we looked a little more closely at this, which is no doubt a notable and alarming characteristic of our time: the number of intelligent men who think and talk despairingly of human nature and of human life. You meet them everywhere. Their books are on your tables. Their talk is in your ears at every corner of the streets. Where has this fact, then, come from if it is, as we believe, the growingly prominent characteristic of our generation? It is not hard to point out some of its sources. Sometimes, with some men, it is a deliberate philosophy. Some of our brightest men have, as I said, really reasoned about the world, and have come to the conclusion that it is bad and not good, and that it is growing worse and not better. It is the issue of all the fatalistic philosophies, and we all know how the strong interest of men in the working of second causes, and in the uniformity of law, has aroused a tendency to fatalism in almost all departments of thinking. Make all life a machine, and the individual is lost; with individual life, goes responsibility; with responsibility, go hope and chance. This is the way in which the philosophical pessimism of our time is made. It begins by the denial of the individual and his free will; and then, with the only power capable of moral goodness taken out, the universe is left unmoral, and an unmoral universe becomes immoral. Its salt is gone and its corruption comes.

But the number of speculative pessimists is small; the number of believers in the badness of the world is large. Where do the rest of them come from? In large part, I believe, from another characteristic of our time, from the strong feeling of interest in, and responsibility for, the world's condition, which comes from the increased activity of mind and conscience, and which begets often narrowness of view about the world's condition. A thousand men today care whether the state is pure, for one who cared in the last century. A thousand eyes are anxiously watching the church, for one that looked to see whether she did her work a hundred years ago. A thousand hearts sink at a catastrophe in the purity of social life, where once only one felt the disgrace. Out of all this watchfulness has come a sensitiveness and a narrowness. Because our own age has its vices which distress us, we forget the vices of other times, and we let ourselves judge the world by that bit of the world which is just under our own eyes. When one thing is being done here in New England, just the opposite thing may be coming to pass on the Ganges or the Nile. Almost every day you hear men assuming that, because America happens to have grown from a very poor country to a very rich one within the last century, and has developed, of course, the vices that belong to wealth, therefore the world is worse today than it was a century ago. It is vastly unreasonable, but it is very natural for a conscientious American to think so. Only when he lifts up his eyes and finds it simply impossible to let them fall on any century in all the world's history which was better than this; any century when government was purer, thought or action freer, society sweeter, the word of man more sacred than it is today, only then does he come back and recognize how he has been allowing the nearness and pressingness of his own circumstances to delude him.

But yet, again, this time of ours, these men of ours, are marked by a singular depth of personal experience. The personal emotions, the anxieties with regard to personal conditions, are very intense. It is a time of much morbidness, and so I think that the danger under which men always labor, of letting the universe take the color of the windows of their own life through which they look at it, was never so dangerous as today. More men today think the world is wretched because they are sad and bewildered, than would have transferred their own conditions to the outside universe in less introspective and self-conscious times. The simplest men in the simplest ages, when they were in sorrow, opened their windows inward to let the world's sunlight in. The elaborate and subtle men in the elaborate and subtle ages, in their sorrow, open their windows outward and darken the bright world with their darkness. And among such men, in such an age, we live.

And one point more. When all these causes, in a time like ours, have set a few earnest, serious, sad men to the hard task of depreciating human life, then it becomes the fashion, and all the light, flippant tongues catch up their cry and repeat it. A few strong men go wrapt in melancholy because they so intensely feel the evil of the world, and straightway every weakling who wants to be thought wise must twist his cloak about his head too, and go stalking tragically among his fellowmen — blind in his mock misery, stumbling over them and making them stumble over him. This was the Byronism of the generation of our fathers, and this is a large part of the pessimism of ours. Sometimes it scowls and frowns and scolds; sometimes it smiles and bows as it declares that religion and politics and social life and personal character are hurrying to ruin; but it is an affectation and a fashion, and is to be discriminated carefully, and set aside in contempt, when we are trying to estimate what there is really respectable and significant in the present defamation of humanity.

Such is a statement of some of the reasons, the principal ones I think, why men have come to talk of their race and its hopes as we very often hear them talk today. They are connected, as you see, with much that is noblest in our age. All together they produce this condition of distrust and fear and wonder about what is coming, with a certain preference for believing that something very bad is coming, with which we are all of us familiar. Men are off their feet, as it were. They are demoralized. There is less readiness to assert the essential nobleness and lofty destiny of man. A state of things like this seems to me to be significant as to where we stand in the world's moral history. We have passed out of the first light-heartedness of youth. We are preparing, by disappointment and bewilderment, for the more serious and earnest satisfactions of middle life. If you recall what I said about the degrees or stages in men's conception of the world's character and prospects, you can apply it now to what I have just been saying. The light and airy optimism which believed that everything was right because the sun shone in the sky, is past for thoughtful mortals. You cannot persuade men today that the world is good because there are many pleasant things in it. They probably never will believe that in the old easy way again. Once having come to see that a pleasant world which is all full of sin and pain, is all the more dreadful because of its outside pleasantness, there is no return to the first easy satisfaction. The only two things that are still open to man are these: a blank despair, which gives itself up to inevitable deterioration; or a new thought of the world as a place of moral training where happiness or unhappiness are accidents, but where, by both happiness and unhappiness, men and nations must be made and can be made just and pure and good.

Which of these two are we bound for? Surely the second, not the first. But to that second we can come only as we keep, in all our bewilderment over the world's misery and sin, the sense, the certainty of God. There is the point of all. If a man dwells upon the misery of human life and does not believe in God, he is dragged down among the brutes. If a man believes in the misery of human life and does believe in God, he is carried up to higher notions of God's government, which have loftier purposes than mere happiness or pain. The one great question about all the kind of temper of which I have spoken is whether it still believes in God. If it does, it must come out in light through whatever darkness it may have first to pass. If it does not, however wise it grows, it certainly must end in folly and despair. Whether our philosophy is theistic or atheistic; whether you, as you look at the snarl of life with all its misery and sin, know for a surety that God is within it all; these are the questions, the answer to which decides whether our philosophy and our observation of life are on their face or on their feet, are full of the curse of despair or full of the blessing of hope.

For all belief in God is, must be, belief in ultimate good. No view of the universe can be despairing which keeps Him still in sight. "Ah," but you say, "do we not all believe in God? Is there one of us that denies His existence?" Probably not; only remember that there is an atheism which still repeats the creed. There is a belief in God which does not bring Him, nay, rather say which does not let Him come, into close contact with our daily life. The very reverence with which we honor God may make us shut Him out from the hard tasks and puzzling problems with which we have to do. Many of us who call ourselves theists are like the savages who, in the desire to honor the wonderful sun-dial which had been given them, built a roof over it. Break down the roof; let God in on your life. And then, however your first light optimism may be broken up, and the evil of the world may be made known to you, you never can be crushed by it. You will stand strong on your feet and hear God when He comes to teach you the lessons of the higher, soberer, spiritual optimism to which they come who are able to believe that all things work together for good to the man or the people that serve Him.

That was the optimism of Jesus. There was no blindness in His eyes, no foolish indiscriminate praise of humanity upon His lips. He saw the sin of that first century and of Jerusalem a thousand times more keenly than you see the sins of this nineteenth century and of America. But He believed in God. Therefore He saw beyond the sin, salvation. He never upbraided the sin except to save men from it. He never beat the chains except to set the captive free; never, as our cynics do, for the mere pleasure of their clanking. "Not to condemn the world, but to save the world," was His story of His mission. And at His cross the shame and hope of humankind joined hands.

O that the truth of our Thanksgiving Day might be His truth; the truth that all the sin we see, all the woe that is around us, are pledges dark and dreadful, but still certain pledges, of man's possible higher life. May I not beg you now to think whether you have been doing wholly right about the matter of which I have spoken to you today? If you have been dwelling solely on the evil that is in man, or on the special evil which you think is in your church, your nation, or your age, see whether that habit has not blinded your intelligence and weakened your strength. It has cast you down upon your face. Stand up, on this Thanksgiving Day, stand up upon your feet! Believe in man! Soberly and with clear eyes believe in your own time and place. There is not, and there has never been, a better time or a better place to live in. Only with this belief can you believe in hope and believe in work. Only to a self-respect which stands erect in conscious privilege, erect for expected duty, can God speak His great and blessed messages and be completely understood.

# The Nearness of God

—⧟—

*That they should seek the Lord, if haply they might feel after him, and find him, though he be not far from every one of us.*

Acts xvii.27

The surprise of life always comes in finding how we have missed the things which have lain nearest to us; how we have gone far away to seek that which was close by our side all the time. Men who live best and longest are apt to come, as the result of all their living, to the conviction that life is not only richer but simpler than it seemed to them at first. Men go to vast labor seeking after peace and happiness. It seems to them as if it were far away from them, as if they must go through vast and strange regions to get to it. They must pile up wealth, they must see every possible danger of mishap guarded against, before they can have peace. Upon how many old men has it come with a strange surprise, that peace could come to rich or poor only with contentment; and that they might as well have been content at the very beginning as at the very end of life. They have made a long journey for their treasure, and when at last they stoop to pick it up, lo! it is shining close beside the footprint which they left when they set out to travel in a circle.

So we seek to know our fellow-men, and think that the knowledge can be gained only by long and suspicious experience and watchfulness of their behavior; but all the while the real power of knowledge is sympathy, and many a child has that, and knows men better than we do with all our cautiousness. And so we plot, and lay our schemes, and go long ways about to make men like us, it may be to be famous, when their liking lies right at our feet; to be ours certainly any moment when we will just be simple and true, and forget ourselves, and genuinely care for other men, and let them see that we care for them in frank and unaffected ways. We try to grow powerful by parading what we think that we can do, by displaying the tools of our power before men, by showing them why they ought to feel our influence. Only gradually we learn that power lies as close to us as work lies, that no man can really do real work and not be powerful.

It is a vague sense of all this, I think, that makes a certain confusion and perplexity and mystery in life. The idea that there is much more near us than we understand or know, that we are every hour on the brink of doing things and being things which yet we never do or are — this is what gives to life a large part of its restlessness, and also a large part of its inspiration. We seem to ourselves, sometimes, like men who are walking in the dark up and down a great, richly furnished house, where tools for every kind of work and supplies for every want are lying on every hand. We find rich things, we taste delicious meats, we recognize the fitness and the care that have provided most ingenious comforts; but all the while we are not sure but there is something even richer, more delicious, more ingenious, which we have almost touched but passed by in the dark.

There comes in life to almost all men, I suppose, a certain sense of fumbling, a consciousness of this vague living in the dark. And out of it there come the everlasting and universal characteristics of humanity, which are in all men of every age and every time, which belong to man as man — the ever reappearing and unquenched hope, the sense that nothing is quite impossible, the discontent with any settled conditions, the self-pity and pathos with which men always regard their own lives when they are thoughtful, and the self-reproach which is always lying in wait just under the surface of our most complacent vanity. All of these — and all of them belong so to human life that the man who has not any of them is an exception — all of them come from that condition in which men vaguely know that they are always missing the things that they need most, that close beside them are most precious

95

things which they are brushing with their robes, which they are touching with their fingers, but which, lying in the dark, they cannot see.

And now suppose that it were possible for any being, standing where he could look at man, apart from him and yet in fullest sympathy with him, to watch his fumbling with a sight that could see through the darkness. What would his feeling be about this humanity that he saw forever missing the helps and chances that it needed, missing them often only by a finger's breadth? How solemn his sight of man would be! Right by the side of our thinking race today lie the inventions and discoveries of the years to come. This seer, to whom the darkness is no darkness, would discern them all. He has always seen how man has missed the nearest things. He saw how for ages the inventions which the world has already reached — the quick-hearted steam, the eager, trembling, vocal electricity, the merciful ether that almost divinely says, "Be still!" to pain — how all these lay unfound just where the hand of man seemed to touch them a hundred times, and then wandered on unwittingly to play with trifles. He saw how a continent lay hid for ages from the eyes of men. He saw how hearts came and went in this world, always just touching on, just missing of, the great comforting truths of a personal immortality, till Christ with His Gospel brought it to light. He has seen how single souls have gone through life burdened, distressed, perplexed, while just beside them, so close that it seemed as if they could not step an inch without seeing it, so close that it seemed as if they could not move without finding their hot and tired soul bathed in its rich waters, flowed the comfortable faith they wanted, the river of the Water of Life which their death was crying out for.

What must be the feeling of such a being about human life? Pity and awe. A blended sense of what a vast endowment man has, what a vast thing it is to be a man, and at the same time of what a terrible thing it is to miss so much — the feeling with which even the weakest child of Gaza looks at the blind giant Samson, helplessly feeling for the great columns of the house. "O Jerusalem, Jerusalem, how often I would have gathered thy children, but thou wouldst not" — Jesus, the Savior, was having just that view of human nature when He cried out so. And who will say that there was not a reverence for Jerusalem mixed with a pity for Jerusalem in the Lord's heart? And when it is not Jerusalem, but you or I, who is not exalted and solemnized when he is able to rise up and believe that there is not merely pity for the sinner who can be so wicked, but reverence for the child of God who might be so good, blended into that perfect unity of Saving Love with which Jesus stoops to lift even the vilest and most insignificant of us out of his sin?

And now, after all this, let us come to our text. St. Paul is preaching on Mars Hill to the Athenians. We hear a great deal about the eloquence, the skill, the tact of that wonderful discourse; of how St. Paul, with exquisite discrimination, said to those men of Athens just the right thing for them. That is putting it too low. The power of his tact was really love. He felt for those men, and so he said to them what they personally needed. And he was, as regarded them, just where the looker-on whom I was picturing is with regard to the men stumbling and fumbling in the darkness of which I spoke. Never were people on the brink of so many of the highest things, and missed them, as these Athenians. They felt all the mystery, the mysterious suggestiveness of life. They built their altar to the unknown God. The air around them was all tremulous with power. They were always on the brink of faith, without believing; always on the brink of divine charity, yet selfish; always touched by the atmosphere of spirituality, yet with their feet set upon the material and carnal. Of such men there were two views to be taken by one who looked in upon their darkness from a higher light. Easy enough it is to be contemptuous; easy enough to cry out "Hypocrite!" to condemn as hopelessly frivolous and insincere this life which always walked on the brink of earnestness, and yet was never earnest; to condemn, as the sweeping critics of all modern doubt are apt to do, every altar to the "Unknown God" as if those who had built it certainly cared more about and worshipped more the "unknown" than the "God," delighted more in His uncertainty than in His Divinity. Easy enough it is to do this, but possible, at least, it is to do something very different from this, possible to be impressed as St. Paul was with reverence and pity that left no room for contempt, reverence for the men who came near to so much, and pity for the men who missed it so sadly. Oh, be sure, my friends, that whenever you see a poor bewildered thinker, or a puzzled youth feeling about vainly for his work, his place, his career in life, there are those two thoughts for you to have about them both — the thought of contempt and the thought of reverence and pity; and be sure that the first thought is mean and unworthy of a fellow-man, and that the second thought is the thought of the best and wisest and divinest men, the thought of St. Paul and of Jesus Christ.

And now, what makes the difference between these two kinds of observation, these two men with their different sight of a human life? It is not hard to see. Is it not simply that the man who looks upon his brother's puzzled life with reverence and pity is the man who sees God there behind the life which he is looking at? The man who looks at his brother's restless life with contempt, is the man who sees no God there, to whom the everlasting human restlessness is nothing but the vain and aimless tossing about of a querulous dissatisfaction. If there is no God whose life and presence, dimly felt, is making men toss and complain, then their tossing and complaining is an insignificant and contemptible thing. It would be better if they could be calm like the beasts. If there is a God to whom they belong, from whom the thinnest veil separates them; whom they feel through the veil, though they cannot see Him; whom they feel through the veil even when they do not know that it is He whom they feel — then their restlessness, their feverish hope, their dreams and doubts, become solemn and significant, something which any thoughtful man may well delight to study, and may well rejoice if he can at all help them to their satisfaction.

And this is just what St. Paul tells the Athenians. He says, "You are restless and discontented. You are always seeming to be near something which yet you do not reach. Your feet are always pressing the brink of a knowledge which you never come to know. You are always half aware of something which you never see. I will tell you what it means. Your restlessness, your impatience, your discontent, however petty be the forms it takes, is solemn and not petty to me, because of what it means. It means that God is not far from every one of you."

Oh, what a revelation that was! What a preaching that was that day on Mars Hill! It was as if one came to a blind child, sitting in a room where he thought himself alone, and wondering at the restlessness which would not let him settle down to quiet thought and work, and said to him, "I can tell you what it means. You are not alone here though you think you are. Your father is here, though you cannot see him. It is his unseen presence that haunts you and disquiets you. All these many disturbances which your mind undergoes are really one disturbance — the single disturbance of his being here. It is simply impossible for you to sit here as if he were not here. The only peace for you is to know and own his presence, to rise up and go to him, to make your whole thought and life center and revolve about the fact that he certainly is here, to quiet your disturbance in the bosom of that presence, known, out of which, unknown, your disturbance came."

And that is what Christianity reveals. What St. Paul said to the men of Athens, Christ says to everybody, to you and me and all these multitudes. He comes to you, and says it: "You are restless, always on the brink of something which you never reach, always on the point of grasping something which eludes you, always haunted by something which makes it impossible for you to settle down into absolute rest. Behold, I tell you what it means. It is God with you. It is Emmanuel. His presence it is that will not let you be at peace. You do not see Him, but He is close by you. You never will have peace until you do see Him and come to Him to find the peace which He will not let you find away from Him. Come unto me, and I will give you rest." That was the revelation of the Incarnation. Listen, how across all the centuries you can hear the Savior giving that revelation, that interpretation of their own troubled lives to multitudes; now to Nicodemus, now to the Samaritan woman, now to Pontius Pilate, and all along, every day, to His disciples by what they saw from hour to hour of His peace in His Father.

Listen again. Hear Christ giving the same revelation today; and ask yourself this: "If it were true, if God in His perfectness, with His perfect standards in Himself, with His perfect hopes for me, God in His complete holiness and His complete love — if He were here close to me, only separated from me by the thin veil of my blindness, would it not explain everything in my life?" There is the everlasting question, my dear friends, to which there is only one answer. What else can explain this mysterious, bewildering, fluttering, hoping, fearing, dreaming, dreading, waiting, human life — what but this, which is the Incarnation truth, that God from whom this life came is always close to it, that He is always doing what He can do for it, even when men do not see Him, and that He cannot do for them all His love would do only because of the veil that hangs between Him and them? "Not far from every one of us!" — there is the secret of our life — weak and wicked because we will not live with God; restless, unable to be at peace in our weakness and wickedness, because God is not far from us.

But it is time for us to take this idea of God very near us, and giving Himself to all of us just as fully as we will receive Him, and follow it out more in detail. God is to men wisdom and comfort and spiritual salvation. See how our truth applies to each of these.

1. And first about God's wisdom. I can conceive of a humanity which, up to the limits of its human powers, should understand God. No cloud should come in anywhere. It should know everything about Him which it was within the range of its nature to comprehend. Then I can conceive of another humanity which should not understand God at all, to which God should not even try to communicate Himself, which He should govern as He governs the unintelligent plants, without an effort to let them know His nature or His plans. Now which of these two is this humanity of ours? Certainly, neither of them. Certainly not the humanity which knows God perfectly, for see how ignorant we are! But certainly, upon the other hand, not the humanity that knows nothing of God; for behold how much we do know, how precious to our hearts is what we know of Him!

What then? I look back over all the history of man's acquaintance with God, all the religions, all the theologies, and it seems to me to be all so plain. Here has been God forever desiring, forever trying, to give the knowledge of Himself to man. There has been never anything like playing with man's mind, like leading men on to ask questions and then wilfully holding back the knowledge which men asked for; always God has been trying to make men understand Him. Never has He turned and gone away in anger, and left man in his ignorance. He has hovered about man's mind with an unbroken presence. Wherever there was any chink, He has thrust in some knowledge of Himself. Thus man in every age, in every condition, even in his own despite, has learned that God is just, that God is merciful, that He governs the world in obedience to His own perfect nature, that He therefore must punish and that He must reward. These are not guesses about God which man has made. They are not beliefs about Him which men have reasoned out from their own natures. They are the truths about Himself which God has been able to press into the human understanding, even through every veil which man drew between himself and God.

I love to think of this; I love to think that there is no man so ignorant, so careless, so indifferent about what God is and what God is doing, that God is not all the time pressing upon that man's life, and crowding into it all the knowledge of Himself that it will take. As the air crowds upon everything, upon the solidest and hardest stone, and on the softest and most porous earth, and into each presses what measure of itself each will receive; so God limits the revelation of Himself by nothing but by the capacity of every man to take and hold His revelation. This is not hard to understand or to believe. Into a roomful of people who differ in natural capacity and education, comes one man whose nature is rich, whom to know is itself a culture. The various people in the room do know him, all of them; but one knows him far more intimately, takes him far more deeply into his understanding, than another. All grades of knowledge about this newcomer are in that room, from almost total ignorance to almost perfect intimacy; but it is not that he has nicely discriminated and determined to whom he shall give himself, to whom he shall deny himself, and just how much he shall give himself to each. He has given the knowledge of himself just as bounteously to each, just as far into each, as he could.

I love to think that that is true of God. The blindest, dullest man is pressed upon by the same knowledge of God, eager to give itself away, that presses on the wisest saint. The man does not wait till our missionary comes to him. You are not kept waiting until all your doubts are settled and your fogs dispersed. At this moment, on every soul in this wide world, God is shedding that degree of the knowledge of Himself which the condition of that soul will allow. Is not that where what we call the false religions come from? They are imperfect religions. If they are religions at all, as indeed they are, it is because of what they know of God. Our missionaries must go to them with our religion as the elder brother goes to the younger brother, speaking of the father, of whom they both know something, out of the fuller knowledge which has come to him, but with sincere respect and reverence for all that his brother has been able to learn already.

Remember, God is teaching you always just as much truth as you can learn. If you are in sorrow at your ignorance then, still you must not despair. Be capable of more knowledge and it shall be given to you. What hinders you from knowing God perfectly is not God's unwillingness but your imperfectness. Grow better and purer, and diviner wisdom shall come to you, not given as wages, as reward, but simply admitted into a nature grown more capable of receiving it. Here is our old text again: "If any man will do his will, he shall know of the doctrine." Here is Christ's old promise again: "Behold, I stand at the door and knock. If any man will open unto me, I will come in and sup with him."

2. But see again how true our truth is when we think of God as the giver not of wisdom, but of comfort. Two men are in deep suffering; the same great woe has fallen upon each of them. They need, with their poor bruised and mangled souls, they both need some healing, some strength which they cannot make for themselves. What is the reason that one of them seems to get it and the other fails? Why is it that one lifts up his head and goes looking at the stars, while the other bends and stoops, and goes with his eyes upon the ground? Is one God's favorite more than the other? Is God near to one and far off from the other? We dream such unhealthy dreams! We fancy such unreal discriminations and favoritisms! We think that one soul is held in the great warm hands, while the other is cast out on the cold ground! But then comes in our truth: "He is not far from every one of us." *From every one of us!* The difference, then, cannot be in God and in His willingness; it must be in the souls.

What, then, can we say to any soul that seems to be left comfortless when other souls all around it are gathering in comfort plentifully? There are two things that we may say, I think; and oh, that I could say them to any of your souls that need them! The first is this: God is comforting and helping you even when you do not know it. Do not let yourself imagine for a moment that God's help to you is limited by what you can feel and recognize. Here is a man upon whom one of the great blows of life has fallen. He is not embittered by it. He is not proud and sullen. He goes to God and knows that his only help is in Him. He goes away and comes back to the same mercy seat, and goes away and comes again; and always he seems to himself to be carrying his whole burden.

He cannot feel it grow any lighter on his shoulders. But all the time he goes about his work. He does his duty. He will not let his sorrow break down his conscience. Do not I know something about that man which he does not know about himself? Do not I know that God is helping him when he thinks himself most unhelped? Do not I know that his burden is a very different thing from what it would be to him if there were no God? Believe and remember that, I beseech you, about your own suffering. If you are really looking to God for help, He is sending you help although you do not know it. Believe it also about your temptation. If you are really asking strength, He is giving you strength, although you do not feel it. Feeling is not the test. Your soul is feeding on it, though your eyes may not see it, any more than they can see the sweet and wholesome air by which you live.

And then, when this is said; and when there still remains the evident difference in the nearness of two men's souls to God which this cannot explain; remember then that the difference must be in the men. In something that you are, not in anything that God is, must be the secret of the darkness of your soul. Do not let yourself for one moment think or feel that God has turned His back upon you, that He has gone away from you and left you to your fate. Don't ask yourself, if He had, who are you that you should call Him back? Who is He that He should turn round at your calling? That way lies despair. No, "He is not far from every one of us." He is not far from you. It is you that must turn to Him; and when you turn His light is already shining full upon you. What a great truth it is, how full of courage, this truth that man may go away from God, but God cannot go away from man! How God loves His own great character of faithfulness! He cannot turn His back upon His child. If His face is not shining upon you, it must be that your back is turned on Him. And if you have turned away from Him, you can turn back to Him again. That is the courage which always comes to one who takes all the blame of life upon himself, and does not cast it upon God. In humility there is always comfort and strength.

3. But we must not stop here. Where is the God who brings the spiritual salvation, who makes a man know his sin, and gives him the blessing of forgiveness and the peace of the new life? Is He, too, near to every man, ready to help, always trying to help all men to be deeply and

spiritually good? This, it seems to me, is what a great many men find it harder to believe than they do that the God of wisdom or comfort is near His children. Many men believe that they can understand God and lay claim to His consolations, who seem to hold that His spiritual presence, the softening, elevating, purifying power of His grace, belongs to certain men only. Indeed, is it not the growing heresy of our time that what we call the Christian character, the beauty of self-sacrifice, devotion, spiritual duty, is possible for some men, but for other men, perhaps for most men, is impossible? That Christian character is not denied; its charm is felt. But it seems to belong to certain constitutions, and to be quite out of the power of others.

Ah, how the human mind swings back forever to a few first ideas, and holds them in some new form in each new age, but does not get beyond them! This feeling about the few men who are supposed to be capable of Christian experience is but the naturalistic statement, in a naturalistic age, of the same idea which in a legal and governmental age was stated as the doctrine of election. The man who, two hundred years ago, would have seen his brethren around him coming to Christ, and have sat down in submissive or sullen misery, saying, "Well, there is no chance for me. Others are called, but I am non-elect" — that same man now, catching the tone of the age, looks round upon the praying and believing multitude, and says more or less sadly, but with no more real self-reproach than the soul which recognized its reprobation: "Religion is a thing of temperament, and I am non-religious." Against them both, protesting that both are false and shallow views of this solemn human life of ours — against them both, whether souls are hiding in them as excuses, or crushed under them as burdens there stands the everlasting simple Bible truth of the universal nearness of God: "He is not far from every one of us."

And just as soon as men really get below the surface, and have broken through the superficial look and current theories of things, and really have come to real study of their own spiritual lives, I believe that it is absolutely true that they always find that there is nothing which so meets the story of their lives, nothing which can so explain themselves to themselves, as this; which you may call at first an hypothesis if you will, but which verifies itself to us as all hypotheses must verify themselves, by the way in which it meets the facts which have to be explained; the hypothesis of God present with and always trying to work upon our souls, to make them good, pure, strong, true, brave; unseen by us, but always close to us; and, because He is God, always working, always hindered by our ignorance, our obstinacy, our wickedness, but never discouraged, never turning away, doing all that omnipotent Love can do upon unwilling human souls to make them live to Him.

If that were true, what would our life be? Think it out; think how a being would live, how he would feel, that was thus ever touched and pressed upon by a God he did not see, trying to persuade him to holiness, trying to convince him of sin; and then run back over the life you have been living ever since you can remember, and tell me if they do not perfectly match and coincide. Restless, self-accusing, dreaming of goodness which you never reached; fitfully trying tasks which all your old experience told you were impossible; haunted by wishes which you dared to laugh at, but did not dare to chase away; with two sets of standards about right and wrong, one which you kept for the world, the other which you hid deep in your heart and were more than half ashamed of — what does all that correspond to but the life that a man must live who is surrounded and pressed upon by an unseen God? God-haunted our lives are, until they give themselves to God, as the brain of a sleeper is haunted by the daylight until he opens his eyes and gives himself a willing servant to the morning.

Or a beast lies tangled in a net. Some kind hands try to unsnarl the cords and let him go. The creature feels them tugging at the strings, and writhes and struggles all the more, and twists himself into a yet more inextricable snarl. But by and by he catches in his dull soul the meaning of the tugs and pulls that he feels, and he enters into sympathy with his deliverers. He lies still while they unbind him, or he moves only so as to help their efforts, and so at last he is free. That is the way in which God sets a soul free from its sins. And therein the soul freed from its sins sees the explanation of all its struggles which have gone before.

This, then, is the story of the present God. What is the meaning of the Incarnation? We picture Christ coming from far, down through the ranks of angels, down from the battlements of heaven; far, far beyond the sun we picture Him leaving His eternal seat and "coming down" to save the world. Then we picture Christ's departure. Back by the way He came, beyond the sun again, once more through the shining hosts, until He takes His everlasting seat at the right hand of God. There is truth in such pictures. But have we not caught more of the spirit of the Incarnation if we think of it, not as the bringing to us of a God who had been far away, but as the showing to us of a God who had been hidden? It is as if the cloud parted and the tired and thirsty traveller saw by his side a brook of clear, sweet water, running along close by the road he travelled. Then the cloud closed again, but the traveller who had once seen the brook never could be faint with thirst again. He must always know where to find it and drink of it. Christ was not a God coming out of absence. He was the ever-present God, revealing how near He always was.

And so of the new life of Christ in man. It is not something strange and foreign, brought from far away. It is the deepest possibility of man, revealed and made actual. When you stand at last complete in Christ, it is not some rare adornments which He has lent from His Divinity to clothe your humanity with. Those graces are the signs of your humanity. They are the flower of your human life, drawn out into luxuriance by the sunlight of the divine Love. You take them as your own, and "wear them as the angels wear their wings."

This is what Belief means, then. Not the far-off search for a distant God, but the turning, the looking, the trusting, to a God who has been always present, who is present now. This is what Belief means. "Believe on the Lord Jesus Christ, and thou shalt be saved."

# The Seriousness of Life

*Let not God speak to us, lest we die.*

Exodus xx.19

The Hebrews had come up out of Egypt, and were standing in front of Sinai. The mountain was full of fire and smoke. Thunderings and voices were bursting from its mysterious awfulness. Great trumpet-blasts came pealing through the frightened air. Everything bore witness to the presence of God. The Hebrews were appalled and frightened. We can see them cowering and trembling. They turn to Moses and beg him to stand between them and God. "Speak thou with us, and we will hear; but let not God speak to us, lest we die."

At first it seems as if their feeling were a strange one. This is their God who is speaking to them, their God who brought them "out of the Land of Egypt, out of the House of Bondage." Would it not seem as if they would be glad to have Him come to them directly, to have Him almost look on them with eyes that they could see, and make unnecessary the interposition of His servant Moses, bringing them messages from Him? Will they not feel their whole history of rescue coming to its consummation when at last they find themselves actually in the presence of the God who has delivered them, and hear His voice?

That is the first question, but very speedily we feel how natural that is which actually did take place. The Hebrews had delighted in God's mercy. They had come singing up out of the Red Sea. They had fol-

107

lowed the pillar of fire and the pillar of cloud. They had accepted God's provision for their hunger. They had received Moses, whom God had made their leader. But now they were called on to face God Himself. In behind all the superficial aspects of their life they were called on to get at its center and its heart. In behind the happy results, they were summoned to deal with the mysterious and mighty cause. There they recoiled. "Nay," they said, "let us go on as we are. Let life not become so terrible and solemn. We are willing to know that God is there. We are willing, we are glad, that Moses should go into His presence and bring us His messages. But we will not come in sight of Him ourselves. Life would be awful. Life would be unbearable. Let not God speak with us, lest we die!"

I want to bid you think this morning how natural and how common such a temper is. There are a few people among us who are always full of fear that life will become too trivial and petty. There are always a great many people who live in perpetual anxiety lest life shall become too awful and serious and deep and solemn. There is something in all of us which feels that fear. We are always hiding behind effects to keep out of sight of their causes, behind events to keep out of sight of their meanings, behind facts to keep out of sight of principles, behind men to keep out of the sight of God. Because that is such poor economy; because the only real safety and happiness of life comes from looking down bravely into its depths when they are opened to us, and fairly taking into account the profoundest meanings of existence; because not death but life, the fullest and completest life, comes from letting God speak to us and earnestly listening while He speaks — for these reasons I think this verse will have something to say to us which it will be good for us to hear.

We have all known men from whom it seemed as if it would be good to lift away some of the burden of life, to make the world seem easier and less serious. Some such people perhaps we know today; but as we look abroad generally do we not feel sure that such people are the exceptions? The great mass of people are stunted and starved with superficialness. They never get beneath the crust and skin of the things with which they deal. They never touch the real reasons and meanings of living. They turn and hide their faces, or else run away when those profoundest things present themselves. They will not let God speak with them. So all their lives lack tone; nothing brave, enterprising, or aspiring is in them. Do you not know it well? Do you not feel it everywhere?

For we may lay it down as a first principle that he who uses superficially any power or any person which he is capable of using profoundly gets harm out of that unaccepted opportunity which he lets slip. You talk with some slight acquaintance, some man of small capacity and little depth, about ordinary things in very ordinary fashion; and you do not suffer for it. You get all that he has to give. But you hold constant intercourse with some deep nature, some man of great thoughts and true spiritual standards, and you insist on dealing merely with the surface of him, touching him only at the most trivial points of living, and you do get harm. The unused capacity of the man — all which he might be to you, but which you are refusing to let him be — is always there, demoralizing you. If you knew that a boy would absolutely and utterly shut his nature up against the high influences of the best men, would you not think it good for him to live not with them but with men of inferior degree, in whom he should not be always rejecting possibilities which he ought to take? A dog might live with a wise man, and remaining still a dog, be all the better for the wise man's wisdom, which he never rejected because he could not accept it. But a brutish man who lived with the sage and insisted that he would be still a brute, would become all the more brutish by reason of the despised and neglected wisdom.

Now we have only to apply this principle to life and we have the philosophy and meaning of what I want to preach to you this morning. It is possible to conceive of a world which should offer the material and opportunity of nothing but superficialness — nothing but the making of money and the eating of bread and the playing of games; and in that world a man might live superficially and get no harm. On the other hand it is possible to conceive of a man who had no capacity for anything but superficialness and frivolity and dealing with second causes; and that man might live superficially even in this deep, rich world in which we live, and get no harm. But — there is the point — for this man with his capacities to live in this world with its opportunities and yet to live on its surface and to refuse its depths, to turn away from its problems, to reject the voice of God that speaks out of it, is a demoralizing and degrading thing. It mortifies the unused powers, and keeps the man always a traitor to his privileges and his duties.

Take one part of life and you can see it very plainly. Take the part with which we are familiar here in church. Take the religious life of man. True religion is, at its soul, spiritual sympathy with, spiritual obedience to God. But religion has its superficial aspects — first of truth to be proved and accepted, and then, still more superficial, of forms to be practised and obeyed. Now suppose that a man setting out to be religious confines himself to these superficial regions and refuses to go further down. He learns his creed and says it. He rehearses his ceremony and practises it. The deeper voice of his religion cries to him from its unsounded depths, "Come, understand your soul! Come, through repentance enter into holiness! Come, hear the voice of God." But he draws back; he piles between himself and that importunate invitation the cushions of his dogma and his ceremony. "Let God's voice come to me deadened and softened through these," he says. "Let not God speak to me, lest I die. Speak thou to me and I will hear." So he cries to his priest, to his sacrament, which is his Moses. Is he not harmed by that? Is it only that he loses the deeper spiritual power which he might have had? Is it not also that the fact of its being there and of his refusing to take it makes his life unreal, fills it with a suspicion of cowardice, and puts it on its guard lest at any time this ocean of spiritual life which has been shut out should burst through the barriers which exclude it and come pouring in? Suppose the opposite. Suppose the soul so summoned accepts the fulness of its life. It opens its ears and cries, "Speak, Lord, for thy servant heareth." It invites the infinite and eternal aspects of life to show themselves. Thankful to Moses for his faithful leadership, it is always pressing through him to the God for whom he speaks. Thankful to priest and church and dogma, it will always live in the truth of its direct, immediate relationship to God, and make them minister to that. What a consciousness of thoroughness and safety; what a certain, strong sense of resting on the foundation of all things is there then! There are no closed, ignored rooms of the universe out of which unexpected winds may blow, full of dismay.

The sky is clear above us, though we have not soared to its farthest height. The ocean is broad before us, though we have not sailed through all its breadth.

Oh, my dear friends, do not let your religion satisfy itself with anything less than God. Insist on having your soul get at Him and hear His voice. Never, because of the mystery, the awe, perhaps the perplexity and doubt which come with the great experiences, let yourself take refuge in the superficial things of faith. It is better to be lost on the ocean than to be tied to the shore. It is better to be overwhelmed with the greatness of hearing the awful voice of God than to become satisfied with the piping of mechanical ceremonies or the lullabies of traditional creeds. Therefore seek great experiences of the soul, and never turn your back on them when God sends them, as He surely will!

The whole world of thought is full of the same necessity and the same danger. A man sets himself to think of this world we live in. He discovers facts. He arranges facts into what he calls laws. Behind his laws he feels and owns the powers to which he gives the name of force. There he sets his feet. He will go no further. He dimly hears the depth below, of final causes, of personal purposes, roaring as the great ocean roars under the steamship which, with its clamorous machineries and its precious freight of life, goes sailing on the ocean's bosom. You say to him, "Take this into your account. Your laws are beautiful, your force is gracious and sublime. But neither is ultimate. You have not reached the end and source of things in these. Go further. Let God speak to you." Can you not hear the answer? "Nay, that perplexes all things. That throws confusion into what we have made plain and orderly and clear. Let not God speak to us, lest we die!" You think what the study of Nature might become, if, keeping every accurate and careful method of investigation of the way in which the universe is governed and arranged, it yet was always hearing, always rejoicing to hear, behind all methods and governments and machineries, the sacred movement of the personal will and nature which is the soul of all. Whether we call such hearing science or poetry, it matters not. If we call it poetry, we are only asserting the poetic issue of all science. If we call it science, we are only declaring that poetry is not fiction but the completest truth. The two unite in religion, which when it has its full chance to do all its work shall bring poetry and science together in the presence of a recognized God, whom the student then shall not shrink from, but delight to know, and find in Him the illumination and the harmony of all his knowledge.

The same is true about all motive. How men shrink from the profoundest motives! How they will pretend that they are doing things for slight and superficial reasons when really the sources of their actions are in the most eternal principles of things, in the very being of God Himself. I stop you and ask you why you give that poor man a dollar, and you give me some account of how his poverty offends your taste, of how unpleasant it is to behold him starve. I ask you why you toil at your business day in and day out, year after year. I beg you to tell me why you devote yourself to study, and you reply with certain statements about the attractiveness of study and the way in which every extension or increase of knowledge makes the world more rich. All that is true, but it is slight. It keeps the world thin. This refusal to trace any act back more than an inch into that world of motive out of which all acts spring, this refusal especially to let acts root themselves in Him who is the one only really worthy cause why anything should be done at all — this is what makes life grow so thin to the feeling of men who live it; this is what makes men wonder sometimes that their brethren can find it worthwhile to keep on working and living, even while they themselves keep on at their life and work in the same way. This is the reason why men very often fear that the impulse of life may give out before the time comes to die, and shudder as they think how awful it will be to go on living with the object and the zest of life all dead. Such a fear never could come for a moment to the man who felt the fountain of God's infinite being behind all that the least of God's children did for love of Him.

I know very well how all this which I have undertaken to preach this morning may easily be distorted and misunderstood. It may seem to be the setting forth of a sensational and unnatural idea of life, the struggle after which will only result in a histrionic self-consciousness, a restless, discontented passion for making life seem intense and awful, when it is really commonplace and tame. "Let us be quiet and natural," men say, "and all will be well." But the truth is that to be natural is to feel the seriousness and depth of life, and that no man does come to any worthy quietness who does not find God and rest on Him and talk with Him continually. The contortions of the sensationalist must not blind us to the real truth of that which he grotesquely parodies. His blunder is not in thinking that life is earnest, but in trying to realize its earnestness by stirring up its surface into foam instead of piercing down into its depths, where all is calm. Yet even he, grotesque and dreadful as he is, seems almost better than the imperturbably complacent soul who refuses to believe that life is serious at all.

The whole trouble comes from a wilful or a blind underestimate of man. "Let not God speak to me, lest I die," the man exclaims. Is it not almost as if the fish cried, "Cast me not into the water, lest I drown," or as if the eagle said, "Let not the sun shine on me, lest I be blind." It is man fearing his native element. He was made to talk with God. It is not death, but his true life, to come into the divine society and to take his thoughts, his standards, and his motives directly out of the hand of the eternal perfectness. Man does not know his own vitality, and so he nurses a little quiver of flame and keeps the draught away from it, when if he would only trust it and throw it bravely out into the wind, where it belongs, it would blaze into the true fire it was made to be. We find a revelation of this in all the deepest and highest moments of our lives. Have you not often been surprised by seeing how men who seemed to have no capacity for such experiences passed into a sense of divine companionship when anything disturbed their lives with supreme joy or sorrow? Once or twice, at least, in his own life, almost every one of us has found himself face to face with God, and felt how natural it was to be there. Then all interpreters and agencies of Him have passed away. He has looked in on us directly; we have looked immediately upon Him; and we have not died — we have supremely lived. We have known that we never had so lived as then. We have been aware how natural was that direct sympathy and union and communication with God. And often the question has come, "What possible reason is there why this should not be the habit and fixed condition of our life? Why should we ever go back from it?" And then, as we felt ourselves going back from it, we have been aware that we were growing unnatural again; we were leaving the heights, where our souls breathed their truest air, and going down into the valleys, where only long habit and an educated distrust of our own high capacity had made us feel ourselves more thoroughly at home.

And as this is the revelation of the highest moments of every life, so it is the revelation of the highest lives; especially it is the revelation of the highest of all lives, the life of Christ. Men had been saying, "Let not God speak to us, lest we die"; and here came Christ, the man — Jesus, the man; and God spoke with Him constantly, and yet He lived with the most complete vitality. He was the livest of all living men. God spoke with Him continually. He never did a deed, He never thought a thought, that He did not carry it back with His soul before it took its final shape and get His Father's judgment on it. He lifted His eyes at any instant and talked through the open sky, and on the winds came back to Him the answer. He talked with Pilate and with Peter, with Herod and with John; and yet his talk with them was silence; it did not begin to make His life, to be His life, compared with that perpetual communion with His Father which made the fundamental conscious-ness as it made the unbroken habit of His life. All this is true of Jesus. You who know the rich story of the Gospels know how absolutely it is true of Him. And the strange thing about it is that the life of which all this is true is felt at once to be the most natural, the most living life which the world has ever seen. Imagine Jesus saying those words which the Hebrews said: "Let not God speak to me, lest I die." You cannot put those words upon His lips. They will not stay there. "O God, speak to me, that I may live" — that is the prayer with which He comes out of the stifling air of the synagogue or the temple, out of the half-death of the mercenary streets, out of the foolish rivalries and quarrelings of His disciples.

And every now and then a great man or woman comes who is like Christ in this. There comes a man who naturally drinks of the fountain and eats of the essential bread of life. Where you deal with the mere borders of things he gets at their hearts; where you ask counsel of expe-diencies, he talks with first principles; where you say, "This will be profitable," he says, "This is right." Remember I am talking about him now only with reference to this one thing — that when men see him they recognize at once that is is from abundance and not from defect of vitality that this man lives among the things which are divine. Is there one such man — it may be one such boy — in the store where all the rest of you are working for rivalry or avarice? Is there one who works from principle, one who works for God; and will you tell me whether you do not all count him the most genuinely living of you all?

The student of history knows very well that there are certain ages and certain races which more than other ages seem to have got down to the fundamental facts, and to be living by the elemental and eternal forces — ages and races which are always speaking with God. So we all feel about the Hebrews. The divine voice was always in their ears. Often they misunderstood it. Often they thought they heard it when it was only the echo of their own thoughts and wishes that they heard; but the desire to hear it, the sense that life consisted in hearing it — that never left them. And so, too, we feel, or ought to feel, about the great Hebrew period of our own race, the Puritan century, in which everything was probed to the bottom, all delegated authorities were questioned, and earnestness everywhere insisted upon having to do immediately with God. Plenty of crude, gross, almost blasphemous developments of this insistence set themselves forth; but the fact of the insistence was and still is most impressive. It never frightened the Puritan when you bade him stand still and listen to the speech of God. His closet and his church were full of the reverberations of the awful, gracious, beautiful voice for which he listened. He made little, too little, of sacraments and priests, because God was so intensely real to him. What should he do with lenses who stood thus full in the torrent of the sunshine? And so the thing which makes the history of the Puritans so impressive is the sense that in them we come close to the great first things. We are back behind the temporary, special forms of living, on the bosom of the primitive eternal life itself.

When we turn suddenly from their time to our own time what a difference there is! At least what a difference there is between all their time and a part of ours. For our time is not capable of being characterized as generally and absolutely as theirs. It has many elements. Certainly it has much of Puritanism. The age which has had Carlyle for its prophet, and which has fought out our war against slavery has not lost its Puritanism. But the other side of our life, how far it is from the first facts of life, from God, who is behind and below everything! When I listen to our morals finding their sufficient warrant and only recognized authority in expediency; when I behold our politics abandoning all ideal conceptions of the nation's life and talking as if it were only a great mercantile establishment, of which the best which we can ask is that it should be honestly run; when I see society conceiving no higher purpose for its activities than amusement; when I catch the tone of literature, of poetry, and of romance, abandoning large themes, studiously and deliberately giving up principles and all heroic life, and making itself the servant and record of what is most sordid and familiar, sometimes even of what is most uncomely and unclean; when I think of art grown seemingly incapable of any high endeavor; when I consider how many of our brightest men have written the word Agnostic on their banner, as if not to know anything, or to consider anything incapable of being known, were a condition to shout over and not to mourn over — when I see all these things, and catch the spirit of the time of which these things are but the exhibitions and the symptoms, I cannot help feeling as if out of this side, at least, of our time there came something very like the echoes of the old Hebrew cry, "Let not God speak to us, lest we die." We are afraid of getting to the roots of things, where God abides. What bulwarks have you, rich, luxurious men, built up between yourselves and the poverty in which hosts of your brethren are living? What do you know, what do you want to know, of the real life of Jesus, who was so poor, so radical, so full of the sense of everything just as it is in God? You tremble at the changes which are evidently coming. You ask yourself, How many of these first things, these fundamental things, are going to be disturbed? Are property and rank and social precedence and the relation of class to class going to be overturned? Oh, you have got to learn that these are not the first things, these are not the fundamental things! Behind these things stand justice and mercy. Behind everything stands God. He must speak to you. He will speak to you. Oh, do not try to shut out His voice. Listen to Him that you may live. Be ready for any overturnings, even of the things which have seemed to you most eternal, if by them He can come to be more the King of His own earth.

And in religion, may I not beg you to be vastly more radical and thorough? Do not avoid, but seek, the great, deep, simple things of faith. Religious people read thin, superficial books of religious sentiment, but do not meet face to face the strong, exacting, masculine pages of their Bibles. They live in the surface questions about how the Church is constituted, how it ought to be governed, what the forms of worship ought to be. They shrink from the profound and awful problems of the soul's salvation by the Son of God and preparation for eternity. Do we not hear — strangest of all! — in religion, which means the soul's relationship to God, do we not hear there — strangest of all — the soul's frightened cry, "Let not God speak with me, lest I die"? In all your personal life, my friends, it is more thoroughness and depth that you need in order to get the peace which if you spoke the truth you would own that you so woefully lack. You are in God's world; you are God's child. Those things you cannot change; the only peace and rest and happiness for you is to accept them and rejoice in them. When God speaks to you you must not make believe to yourself that it is the wind blowing or the torrent falling from the hill. You must know that it is God. You must gather up the whole power of meeting Him. You must be thankful that life is great and not little. You must listen as if listening were your life. And then, then only, can come peace. All other sounds will be caught up into the prevailing richness of that voice of God. The lost proportions will be perfectly restored. Discord will cease; harmony will be complete.

I beg you who are young to think of what I have said to you today. Set the thought of life high at the beginning. Expect God to speak to you. Do not dream of turning your back on the richness and solemnity of living. Then there will come to you the happiness which came to Jesus. You, like Him, shall live, not by bread alone, but by every word that proceedeth out of the mouth of God!

# The Transfiguration of Christ

—ɯ—

*And Peter answered and said to Jesus, Master, it is good for us*
*to be here: and let us make three tabernacles; one for Thee,*
*and one for Moses, and one for Elias. For he wist not what to*
*say.*

Mark ix.5, 6

In that book which is known as the Second Epistle of St. Peter, the
apostle, now grown into old age, is heard recalling the event of
which the story is told in this chapter of St. Mark. "And this voice
which came from heaven," he says, "we heard when we were with Him
in the holy mount." He is remembering the Transfiguration. Through
all the busy and burdened years which have come in between, Peter has
never ceased to hear that voice which on the mountain had declared Jesus to be "the beloved Son of God." As he looked back to the whole
scene he must have been thankful that his impulsive suggestion, spoken in the confusion, when "he wist not what to say," had not been accepted by his Lord. The event which he remembered had been so much
more to him than if its outward form had been made perpetual. It had
passed into that glorified world of memory, where its spiritual meaning and radiance had shone out from it. It had become sacred forever
with the manifestation of its spiritual truth.

This is the best thing which can happen to the events of life: that
they should pass into the region of exalted memory, where their true

118

light may shine out for the illumination of all the life which we have yet to live. Less and less, I think, do we desire that the mere conditions and circumstances of life should be maintained. More and more do we dread that the events of the past should be lost out of our memory. Richer and richer seems to be that illumination in which they are set when they are spiritually remembered and we can see the fullness of their meaning. It is not always pleasant to see still standing on the street-side the house in which you lived when you were a boy. Other people have come and lived in it, and their lives, mixed with yours, look out upon you from its windows. But your boyhood itself — that goes back from you into a realm of light and eternity, winning clearness and interpretation as it goes, and takes its place there, glorified, not distorted, revealed, not falsified, pouring out power and illumination upon all your life. As the great men of the world walk sometimes with great labor and distress along the common streets of life and then pass off into a world of undying fame, where they stand close and clear forever to the heart and the intelligence of man, so the great events of our lives have their world of undying influence, whence their power comes forth to touch and shape the life which is made up of the procession of less illustrious events.

I want to speak to you today of the power of the most exalted moments of our lives. The Transfiguration had been the most splendid moment in the life of Peter. Part of his life had been lived in the commonplace labor of his trade as fisherman. Part of it had been given to the loving and puzzled study of his Master's nature, trying to find out the secret of this wonderful power. One long stretch of it had been clouded with his mean and wretched sin. Many years of it had been given to the patient, faithful labor of his missionary life. In the midst of it all there shone forth one experience of unmixed and certain glory. Out of this confused and undulating land stood up one mountain-top which never lost the light. Once he had seen Jesus in apocalyptic glory. Once he had felt the very fire which burns in the robes of the everlasting purity and power. Once every doubt, every darkness, every delay, had disappeared, and he had been in heaven for an hour. The splendor of that moment never faded. The old man died rejoicing in the memory that it had once been his, and feeling sure that in it was the promise of all the glory to which he was going.

To many, if not to all, men's lives come such splendid moments as came to Peter on the mountain of the Transfiguration. If I could uncover the hearts of you who are listening to me this morning I think that I should find in almost all — perhaps in all — of them a sacred chamber where burns the bright memory of some loftiest moment, some supreme experience, which is your transfiguration time. Once on a certain morning you felt the glory of living, and the misery of life has never since that been able quite to take possession of your soul. Once you knew for a few days what was the delight of a perfect friendship. Once you saw for an inspired instant the idea of your profession blaze out of the midst of its dull drudgery. Once, just for a glorious moment, you saw the very truth and believed in it without the shadow of a cloud. Do not you know some of these experiences? I am sure you do. And often the question must have come, "What do they mean? What value may I give to these transfiguration times?" So much depends upon the answer which we give to that question that I may well ask you to study it with me awhile.

And, first of all, the impulse must be right which gives to these highest experiences of our lives a prophetic value. The first instinct is to feel that they are not complete and final; that they point to something which is yet to come; that they are the premonitions, the anticipations, of a fuller condition, in which that which they manifested fitfully and transiently shall become the constant and habitual possession of the life.

What a mockery there would be in these supreme ecstatic moments of life if they did not meet with this instinct and claim their interpretation from it! Once to have been brought up out of the dungeon and shown the sunlight and then be carried back again, and, with the memory of it still in our eyes, to hear the bolt driven and the key thrown into the depths, so that we never again could be released one moment from our darkness — what wretchedness could equal that! Once to have seen for a moment what it is to believe, and then to feel the stone of unbelief rolled hopelessly to our tomb door — all the convictions of the human soul stand up against a cruel mockery like that! It cannot be!

And these convictions of the human soul find manifold support in what men see on many sides. There are abundant instances in which some splendor which is by and by to become fixed and habitual shows itself first in a sudden splendid flash of light, which disappears the moment it has showed itself to the man's astonished eyes. When was ever any invention made which ultimately was to take its quiet place in the midst of the prosperous industry of humankind, but first it showed itself as a dream and vanished like an impossibility before the eyes of some amazed, ingenious youth, who hopelessly begged that it would stay with him, and wist not what he said? The motive which by and by, with its steady pressure, is going to move all our life is felt first like a wayward gust out of some transcendental, unimaginable world. The friend who is to be our life's unfailing solace appears to us first in some garment of light, which we can only reverence at a distance, and can never dare to touch. It is the most familiar testimony of all truly thoughtful men. That which is ultimately to become the soul's habitual support comes first in some supreme exceptional manifestation, which, even though it disappears, still leaves behind it in man's instincts a memory that is full of hope, a deep conviction that it has not gone forever, and so a strength to watch and wait and hope for its return.

It seems to me like this: A traveler is going through a country by a long straight road which leads at last to a great city which is his final goal. At the very beginning of the journey the road leads over a high hill. Up on the summit of that hill the traveler can clearly see the spires of the far-away city flashing in the sun. He feasts his eyes on it. He fills his eyes with it. And then he follows the road down into the valley. It loses the sight of the city almost immediately. It plunges into forests. It sounds the depths in which flow the dark waters which the sun never touches. But yet it never forgets the city which it saw from the hilltop. It feels that distant unforgotten glory drawing it toward it in a tight straight line. And when at last the traveler enters in and makes that city thenceforth his home, it is not strange to him, because of the prophecy of it which has been in his heart ever since he saw it from the hill.

If we read rightly, thus, the method by which God brings His children to their best attainment, it is certainly a method full of wisdom and beauty. First, He lets shine upon them for a moment the thing He wants them to become, the greatness or the goodness which He wishes them to reach. And then, with that shining vision fastened in their hearts, He sets them forth on the long road to reach it. The vision does not make it theirs. The journey is still to be made, the battle is still to be fought, the task is still to be done. But all the time, through the long process, that sight which the man saw from the mountain-top is still before the eyes, and no darkness can be perfectly discouraging to him who keeps that memory and prophecy of light.

A memory which is not also a prophecy is terrible. Better to forget than to remember only as a thing that is past and finished forever. You recall the happy days of an old friendship. Unless it is a perpetual revelation to you of the perfect friendship of the perfect life it comes to be a torture.

"'Tis better to have loved and lost/Than never to have loved at all," but the true blessedness is reached only when you know that that which you have seen plunged into the fiery furnace is to come out again, the same, but finer, purer, holier, more worthy of the child of God!

When we have really grasped this truth, then how interesting and impressive becomes the sight of the life of our fellow-men! Many and many of these men whom we see plodding on in their dusty ways are traveling with visions in their souls. Nobody knows it but themselves and God. Once, years ago, they saw a light. They knew, if only for a moment, what companionships, what attainments, they were made for. That light has never faded. It is the soul of good things which they are doing in the world today. It makes them sure when other men think their faith is gone. It will be with them till the end, until they come to all it prophesies.

Childhood, coming at the beginning of every life, is in the lives of many men this time of vision and of prophecy. We live in those first years in which it seems easy to do and be great things. We are full of the sense of God. We are surrounded by an atmosphere of faith. And then come doubt and hardship and the falseness of men. Tell me, who is there of us that could live through it all if we had not been upon the mountain-top first and seen and believed? There is not the skeptic who once prayed as a little child that is not to the end of his skeptical life the better for that prayer. There is not the cynic, despising and despairing of his brethren, who has not at the bottom of his heart the seed of a better hope, kept from the days when as a boy he trusted them and knew that in every one of them was a capacity of goodness.

If we go a little deeper into the philosophy of this power which belongs to the memory of our best moments, if we ask ourselves why it is that God has appointed such a treatment as I have been trying to describe for His children, I think we are not wholly at a loss. May it not be that in this way a condition or conviction which in the first place took its shape under special circumstances may best become an independent spiritual possession of the soul, to be used in all the various circumstances of the life? You cast a tool of iron in a mold. Then you break the mold and throw it away; but the tool which first took shape in it stays in your hand and is yours for a hundred uses. So, suppose that years ago there came some crisis in your life which taught you the necessity and the glory of being brave. It was some mighty day of God with you. With lightnings and thunderings God scattered your timid fears and made your whole masculine vigor to come forth. You dared to fight because you dared not feebly run away. It was a revelation of you to yourself. What then? The crisis past, the lightnings faded and the thunders hushed, you came down from the mountain. Ever since that you have walked on in quiet, level ways. But many a time, in simple tasks which had not power of themselves to bring you such self-revelations, you have found yourself able to be brave with a bravery whose possibility you learned in that tremendous hour. If, had your life continued in that tumult, you would have come to think that bravery belonged to tumult and was only possible in the stress of battle, can you not see why God caused the sky of your life to clear, and would not let you build your tabernacle on the mountain? Now you are brave for any lot. Your courage, summoned by some petty struggle of today, does not even recall the first awakening which came to it in that long-past exalted hour. Men are meeting the petty enemies of the household and the street today with a fortitude and a fearlessness which they learned thirty years ago on the battlefields of the Rebellion. Men are bearing little disappointments with a patience which was born in them while they stood by the death-bed of their best beloved and watched the hopes of all their life slowly sink under the rising flood. It is good that the power which is first born under exacting and peculiar circumstances should then be set free from those circumstances altogether and become the general possession of the life, available for all its needs. The cloud forms about the mountain-peak; but once formed there, it floats away and drops its blessing upon many fields.

Closely resembling this is the way in which the qualities of great men become the possession of the world. Great men are in the world what the most enlightened and exalted experiences are in the life of any man. They are the mountain-tops on which the influences which are afterward to fertilize our whole humanity have birth. There stands out some great pattern of unselfishness; some martyr-life which totally forgets itself and lives in suffering self-sacrifice for fellow-men. About that man's life gathers an utterance, an exhibition, of the glory of self-sacrifice — of how it is the true life of mankind, of how in it alone man becomes truly man. Does all that abide in him, live and die in his single personality? Does it disappear forever in the withering flames which consume him at the stake? Does not that fire set it free, cast it forth into the atmosphere of the universal human nature, and make it the possession of all mankind? Have not you and I the power to live more unselfishly today because of the unselfishness of the great monumental lives of devotion?

What is the power of the cross of Jesus? Manifold, I am sure; more manifold than you or I, or all the sinners who have been saved by it, or all the theologians who have devoutly studied it in all the ages, have begun to know or tell. But certainly one part of its power lay here: it was the loftiest manifestation of man's power to give himself for duty and for fellow-man that the earth has ever seen. In Jesus our humanity went up into the mountain and was transfigured. It shone with light there on the cross. Thenceforth, into whatever depths of selfishness it might descend, it carried the power of that transfiguration with it. In its certainty that He who suffered there was one with it and really bore its nature, it knew that not to be selfish, but to be unselfish, was its true life. That is the reason why so wonderfully, through all the years of miserable self-seeking which have come since, souls everywhere have come out under the power of that cross and let themselves be crucified for fellow-men, and why the dream of a world glorious with mutual devotion has never been lost out of men's hearts.

Those lives of self-devotion, however humble and obscure they seem, have always themselves the same power which belongs to the sacrifice of Jesus. They too throw light on darker lives. They are lesser hill-tops grouped around the great mountain. Such lives may we live in any little world where God has set us!

The most interesting and suggestive groups in the world are always those in which identity and contrast are most fitly mingled. A scene of nature gives us the best pleasure when it is like and yet unlike some scene which we have seen before; not its mere duplicate, and, on the other hand, not so entirely different from it as to suggest no comparison. Two men call forth our interest when they both are evidently human, making us feel the humanity which is common to them both, and yet each has his distinct peculiarities and personal characteristics. Is not this the principle which really is at the heart of our relation to the exalted and triumphant moments of our past life? What is it that makes a man plodding along through regions of prosaic doubt remember always one shining day of years ago, when all the clouds of doubt parted and swept away, and for the time he thoroughly believed? It is because of the sense of identity and the sense of contrast both, which the remembrance of that day brings with it. In the midst of all his bewilderment he feels sure that he is the same man who lived that glorious, ecstatic day. It is not another man's. It is his. And in all the exultant sense of its possession he is all the more terribly aware how far he has departed from it now. It fills his present life with shame. These two together blend into the longing regard with which he looks back upon it, into the eager tenacity with which he treasures it. If there were no sense of contrast with the present, that long-past day of loftier experience would fade away, and the man would live in the mere satisfaction of immediate delight. If there were no sense of identity the degenerate present would seem to be the soul's only condition. The happier past would seem to belong to some other man, and so no hope would flow out from it to the prostrate life, promising it better things.

Is not this so? Years, years ago, it may be, God gave you a day of exalted communion with Himself. Perhaps in connection with some particular event of suffering or joy, perhaps entirely apart from anything which happened, as if God gave it directly out of His opened hand, God sent you a longer or a shorter period of calm, profound, spiritual peace and joy. It was full of assurance. God seemed very real and very near to you. His truth was not only easy to believe, you hungered after more of it. You went seeking for more that you might know of Him. You did not need to seek for Him; you found Him everywhere. Christ and His light shone out from everything. As you remember those days you have no doubt of their reality. They are the realest days of all your life. They keep a hold on you which will not let you go. And are not these the two hands with which they hold you — the identity and the contrast of your present life? "I, I, this same I, am the man who once lived near to God"; and "Lo, how far from God, in what a desert of worldliness and selfishness, I am living now!" The past, our own best past, holds us with these two hands and will not let us go.

No doubt there is a deeper truth about it all. Follow out this truth, and it is impossible for us to stop short of that idea of our self which is in the heart of God and with which He made us to conform. That is what really holds us. It is that from which we cannot get away. It is our identity and our contrast with that which, mingled together, makes the restlessness, the shame, the aspiration of our lives. That "purpose of God concerning us," underlying our lives all the while, breaking forth like subterranean fire at the thinnest spots, taking possession of our consciousness at its most exalted points, as the flame pours out from Vesuvius — that is what really declares itself in our transfiguration times.

That idea of them makes those times most gracious in our history, and perfectly explains the fascination for us which they never lose. They are the utterance of our highest, truest possibility. They are not brilliant unaccountable exceptions. They are our normal life. They are the type of what we always might and ought to be. For the exceptionalness of an event is not properly measured by its rarity. The exception is the departure from the law of life, whether it comes rarely or comes often. If the law of a man's life, the standard, the ideal of it, is that he shall be true, and ninety-nine times today he lies and only once he tells the truth, those ninety-nine times are really ninety-nine exceptions. Once, only once, he has been his true self, conformed to his law.

It is really the feeling of this — to put the matter in a little different way from that in which we have put it before — it is the feeling of this truth that our best moments are not departures from ourselves, but are really the only moments in which we have truly been ourselves, which has made the memory of men's best moments hold them with such power. Those moments became the rallying-points of all their struggles after better life. Every enterprising experience turned to them as to a burning light, drank from them as from a living fountain. They gave unity to all the scattered struggles. This and that effort to resist temptation was not a solitary thing, sure, in its solitariness, to fail and disappear. They were signs of the nature struggling for its true destiny, the destiny which had been declared and recognized as its truest in that one supreme experience.

All this must have come to Simon Peter. Between the Transfiguration time and the time of his Epistle he had lived in the struggle for holiness and usefulness. Sometimes he had succeeded. Whenever he had had success in any degree, that success must have realized itself in the light of his great memory. Whatever he did that was true and brave must have most easily naturalized itself, so to speak, in virtue of the revelation which had come to him upon the holy mount, that not darkness, but light, not evil, but good, not uselessness, but usefulness, is the true and native condition for a human soul.

If all the world could know that, what a great change would come! If we could all be sure that our best is our most natural — that it is the evil which is most unnatural; if I knew man simply in his intrinsic nature, nothing at all of this long dark history of his, I think that nothing he could do would be so good as to surprise me. It would be his wickedness that would seem strange. To keep that feeling about him, in spite of this long history of his — that is the triumph of the truest faith.

The best men are the truest men. This patience, this courage, this spirituality which makes my friend's life or the world's hero's life sublime and glorious, is not a departure from humanity, it is a realization of humanity. When we look at it we want to say, not, "How strange that a man should be this!" Rather we want to say, "How strange that any man should be anything but this!"

"Christ is the perfect man," we say. When we say that we ought to mean that Christ is the only absolutely true man that has ever lived; that all men, just as far as they fall short of Christ, fall short of humanity; that not that Jesus should be sinless, but that every other human being who ever lived should be a sinner, is the real moral wonder of the world.

Here, and here only, can come the real meaning of the sinfulness of sin. Let me go about always saying to myself, "To err is human!" and what chance is there that I, being conscious of and rejoicing in my humanity, should think it terrible to do what I believe no man can be human without doing? Somebody meets me and says, "Christ!" "Ah, yes," I answer; "but then, you know, He was a peculiar sort of man. He was not just man like us! We cannot think that we can be what He was. That would be to degrade His divinity and to depreciate His work." So we talk with a false show of reverence, when really just the opposite is true. Really we disown and misinterpret Christ when we refuse to see in Him the true type of man, once seeing which no man has any right to be satisfied or rest until he comes to be like Him. That is the real power of His redemption.

The best man is the truest man. It is in our best moments, not in our worst moments, that we are most genuinely ourselves. Oh, believe in your noblest impulses, in your purest instincts, in your most unworldly and spiritual thoughts! It is the moment when the idea of your profession flashes on you through its dry drudgery — that is the moment when you see your occupation the most truly. Believe that, O mercenary merchants, O clerks and shop-boys overwhelmed and stunned by the clamorous detail of business life! You see man most truly when he seems to you to be made for the best things. Believe that, O cynics! May God show it to your blinded eyes. You see your true self when you believe that the best and purest and devoutest moment which ever came to you is only the suggestion of what you were meant to be and might be all the time. Believe that, O children of God!

This is the way in which a soul lives forever in the light which first began to burn around it when it was with Jesus in the holy mount!

# The Tree of Life

—ᴍ—

*And he placed at the east of the garden of Eden Cherubims, and a flaming sword which turned every way, to keep the way of the tree of life.*

Genesis iii.24

The recent discussions about, and criticisms of, the first chapters of the Book of Genesis have left a certain vague and uncomfortable feeling in the minds of many men. Not a few people, probably, think in a dim sort of way that geology, or something else, has made those chapters of very doubtful worth. The worst part of this feeling is that it robs the early story of our race of the spiritual power that it possesses. Apart from the question of its historic character, the account of man's origin which is given in Genesis is profoundly true to man's spiritual experience, and its imagery is representative of perpetual and universal truth. Among its images one of the most prominent and striking is this one of the "tree of life." Let us try, with the beautiful words of the Genesis-story fresh in our minds, to see if we can get at the meaning of it, and understand what is meant by the history of the tree of life which runs through all the Bible.

Let us briefly recall the story. In the garden where God first placed man, the scene of his earliest experiences, it is said that God, his Creator, planted two trees. There were many others, but these two were noticeable and distinct. One of them was the tree of the knowledge of good and evil, and the other was the tree of life. There they stood side by side, both beautiful, both tempting. But on one of them — the most tempting — a prohibition is laid. Of the tree of knowledge man must not taste. But man rebels, wilfully, independently, against God's word, and does eat of the tree. The consequence is that he is not allowed to eat of the other tree. He is driven out of the garden where it stands, and is forbidden to return; and his return is made impossible by "cherubims, and a flaming sword which turned every way, to keep the way of the tree of life."

Thus begins the long career of humanity. Man is forced to undertake the work and drudgery of living. The centuries, laden with wars and pains and hopes and fears and disappointments and successes, start on their slow procession. But no more is heard of the tree of life. It is not mentioned again in the course of the Bible. It is left behind the closed gate and the flaming sword, until we are surprised, at the extreme other end of the Bible, the New Testament, to see it suddenly reappear. In the book of St. John's Revelation, where the promises of the world's final glory are gathered, this promise stands among the brightest: "To him that overcometh will I give to eat of the tree of life, which is in the midst of the Paradise of God." The long-lost tree is not lost after all. God has only been keeping it out of sight; and at last He brings man to it and tells him to eat his fill. "In the midst of the street of it and on either side of the river, was there the tree of life, which bare twelve manner of fruits, and yielded her fruit every month; and the leaves of the tree were for the healing of the nations." Into this glory the angels of God are to bring His people at the last.

This is the story. And now, what does it mean? Certainly nobody can read it and not be sure that the element of allegory is very large in it. Whatever literal events may correspond to it at the beginning or at the end of the human history, certainly that losing and finding again of the tree of life may be taken to represent the course of man's career in spiritual things, the way in which the race and the individual are trained and punished and rewarded. That interpretation, at least, is open to us, because that meaning of the story finds its commentary in our own experience, and in all the history of mankind. If we can understand that meaning, we have reached some idea of the purpose for which the revelation of the Book of Genesis was given.

And that meaning is not hard to find. The tree of life evidently signifies the fulness of human existence — that complete exercise of every power, that roundness and perfectness of being which was in God's mind when He made man in His own image. It represents not mere endurance, not merely an existence which is going to last forever. It represents quality more than quantity, or quantity only as it is the result of quality. To eat of the tree of life is to enter into and occupy the fulness of human existence, to enjoy and exercise a life absolute and perfect, to live in the full completeness of our powers. We can feel, I think, how this luxuriousness and fulness is naturally embodied under the figure of a tree. In many myths of many races, the tree has seemed the fittest symbol of the life of man; and the tree perfect in God's garden is the truest picture of man's whole nature complete under His care.

On the other hand, the tree of the knowledge of good and evil represents that mottled and mingled experience of life by which men's lives are formed, their understandings opened, their characters decided. To eat of the tree of knowledge of good and evil — what is it but to go through just what you and I have gone through ever since we were children? It is to deal with life; to come, by contact with the world, to judgments of what is good and what is bad; to form habits of thinking and ways of feeling about men and women and about their actions. In one word, to have had experience is to have eaten of the tree of the knowledge of good and evil. The little, irresponsible child has never tasted it. It is its savor in the grown man's mouth which gives his face its soberness, and oftentimes its bitterness.

What, then, is the truth about these trees? He who wilfully and rebelliously, in his own way and not in God's way, eats of the tree of knowledge, he shall be shut out from the tree of life. He who wantonly, selfishly, and by the dictates of his own appetites, uses his powers and wins his experience, shall not come to the fulness of those powers, nor get the best out of life. He who insists on knowing things or doing things away from God, shall not rise to the completest capacity of skill or strength or knowledge. Wilfulness, selfishness, independence, self-confidence, shut man out from the perfection of his life.

131

And one point more. Adam and Eve being thus driven out from the tree of life, who were the guards that stood to hinder their return? Cherubims, and a flaming sword which turned every way. And the cherub in Scripture is a being with a certain symbolic character. He is ordinarily represented as a composite creature-form, as a winged man or a human-headed beast — a way to represent that combination of intelligence and force which was also expressed in the Egyptian sphynx and in the winged bulls and lions of Assyria. The essential idea of the cherubims seems to have been that they represented the forces of nature as the servants of God. "The Lord sitteth between the cherubims, be the earth never so unquiet," says David, and in another psalm, "He rode upon a cherub and did fly." These forces of nature, these things of the world about us, these objects and circumstances, made by God to assist in the pleasure and culture of mankind — these same things they are which, when man is rebellious and selfish, stand between him and his fullest life. Those objects and circumstances which, if a man were docile and humble and lived his life with and under God, would all be developing and perfecting him, making him stronger, making him happier — all those things, just as soon as a man cuts himself off from God and insists on getting knowledge and doing work by himself, become his enemies. They hinder him instead of helping him; they are always pulling him down instead of lifting him up; making him a worse and smaller instead of a better and larger man.

Now, follow on with the parable. Man has been driven out, and the cherubims are keeping guard. The tree of life disappears from man's sight, but it is not lost. Man is driven out of the garden where it stands, but immediately the education begins which, if he will submit to it, is to bring him back at last to the Paradise of God where the tree of life will be restored to him. And all the training that comes in between is of one sort. Everything from Genesis to Revelation has one purpose — to teach men the hopelessness, the folly, the unsatisfactoriness, of a merely wilful and selfish life; to bring men by every discipline of sorrow or joy to see the nobleness and fruitfulness of obedience and consecration. When that is learned, then the lost tree reappears. Hidden through all the lingering centuries, there it is, when man is ready for it, blooming in the Paradise of God.

Is not the meaning of that symbol plain? Is not the truth it teaches worthy of a revelation? The highest, fullest life of man has ceased to be actual upon the earth. You cannot find one man who is living it, not one who, in some part of his nature or his conduct, is not pinched and meagre, missing the completeness for which he was made. But the possibility of that highest life never has been lost. It is waiting till man is able to reclaim it. And man shall reclaim it just as soon as he is completely in harmony with and obedient to God.

One other point comes in — not very clearly, but with a suggestion that completes the picture. Again and again in Scripture we read of the angels as God's agents in the restoration of His people to their long-lost glory. "The reapers are the angels," in the mighty harvest. The beggar Lazarus, after all his waiting and wretchedness was over, was "carried by the angels into Abraham's Bosom." And the angels are said to watch with joy as each new repentant sinner claims forgiveness and, being forgiven, returns into harmony with God and into his possibility of perfectness. It is not clearly said, but if, among these rescuing and helping angels, there are found the cherubims who were set to guard the gate of the first Paradise against the unhappy man's return — then, the whole story is complete. It is by those same forces of nature which are now his hindrances that man is finally to overcome. Not by a new dispensation, not by a new world of things, but by these same things, these very same old things which have so long stood between him and his highest, he is finally to reach his highest. The cherubims who so long shut him out from, are at last to bring him back to, the tree of life.

This is the story of the world then, and the story of man as the Bible tells it — the story of the lost and refound tree of life. There is something broad and primal in that universal figure of the tree. It is interesting, I think, to turn to the New Testament and see how, when Jesus Christ came, the story which He had to tell of man's condition and prospects was just the same with this old story of the tree of Genesis. Take the parable of the prodigal son — how different it is! how quiet and domestic and familiar! how homely in its quaint details! But if you look at it, you will see that the meaning is the same. There, too, there is a first native possibility, the place in the father's house to which the boy was born. There, too, that possibility ceases to be actual because of the wilfulness of him to whom it was offered. "Give me the portion of goods that falleth to me"; it is exactly Adam and Eve over again. There, too, the possibility is not destroyed, but stands waiting, out of sight of the wanderer, but always expecting his return; the father's house from which the son goes out, and which stands with its door open when long afterwards he comes struggling back. There, too, the instant that submission is complete — "I will arise and go to my father" — the lost possibility is found again, for, "While he was yet a great way off, his father saw him and ran and fell on his neck and kissed him." The story of the tree of life and the story of the prodigal son are the same story. Drawn with such different touch, colored in such different hues, they set before us still the same picture of the life of man.

It might be well to look at that picture as it represents the world's life, and as it represents the life of the individual. I shall only undertake to do the latter. Of the other let me merely remind you in a few words how true a conception, how complete an explanation, of the state of things which we see everywhere around us is this great Bible conception of the hidden tree of life. It is not lost, not totally destroyed forever, not taken out of man's hope — that better possibility of man, that full condition of humanity, in which every act has its most perfect motive, and every motive its most perfect act. It is not lost, but it is hidden; hidden where the powers of the world will not let men get at it, but where men feel that it exists, live otherwise than they would live if they knew that it had perished, and never give over the hope of reaching it some day again.

Could any picture more completely describe this mixed state of the world we live in? The alternations of hope and despair, the way that generosity and meanness by turns take possession of the world, the wars and tumults, the eagerness for progress and the dreary clinging to old sins, the history of the world for any one week, the passions that agitate the breast of any ruler, the motives and feelings that contend in a political convention — where is there any theory of man that takes them all in more perfectly than this Bible theory of the tree of life; lost but not destroyed, blooming somewhere still behind the cherubims, never quite forgotten, and to be made visible again when man shall have become able, by long education, to enter in and take of its fruit and eat?

134

But let us leave this larger view, and turn to see how, in the life of each of us, the story of the tree of life finds its fulfilment. Every man has his tree of life — the full completeness of life for him, the best that those powers which he has, that special combination of qualities that he is, is capable of being. It gives a dignity to every human being to think this of each. It breaks the herd and sets the individual before you. Walk down the crowded street some day, and think of it. They all look so alike, these men and women, such hosts of them, with the same narrow, vulgar, greedy faces! They sweep by you as little distinguished as the drops in the stream that goes hurrying and whirling past your feet.

But think of them again. Every man and woman of them has a tree of life — a separate completeness of character, a possibility which, if he could fulfil it, would stand a distinct and perfect thing in the universe, the repetition of no other that ever went before, and never to be repeated by any that shall come after. Take out the meanest and most sordid face that passes you, the face most brutalized by vice, most pinched and strained by business — that man has his tree of life, his own separate possibility of being, luxuriant and vital, fresh, free, original. "How terribly he has missed of it," you say. Indeed he has. A poor, undistinguishable thing he is, as wretched as poor Adam when he had been driven from his tree of life, and stood naked and shivering outside the Garden, with the beasts that used to be his subjects snarling at him, and the ground beginning to mock him with its thorns and thistles. That poor man evidently has been cast out of his garden, and has lost his tree of life. And is it not evident enough how he lost it? Must it not have been that he was wilful? Must it not have been that, at the very beginning, he had no idea but for himself, no notion of living in obedience to God? Do not say that that is a false and artificial explanation, a mere minister's sermon explanation of how this insignificant creature on the street lost all his chance of a strong, vital life. Tell me, nay, ask yourself, if he had realized God, if he had known and been glad to know from the beginning that his life belonged to God, if he had really tried to serve God, could he have come to this? If consecration could have saved him, is it not the absence of consecration that has ruined him?

And he is only a single emphasized and recognizable example. All the failures of men are of the same sort. What makes the scholar's life a failure? What makes him sigh when at last the books grow dim before his eyes, and the treacherous memory begins to break and lose the treasures it has held? He has been studying for himself, wilfully, not humbly, taking the fruit from the tree of knowledge. What makes the workman turn into a machine? What makes us feel so often, the more his special skill develops, that he is growing less and not more a man? What shuts the merchant up to his drudgery, making it absolutely ridiculous and blasphemous to say of him, as we watch the way he lives and the things he does from the time he rises till the time he goes to bed, "That is what God made that man for"? What makes every one of us sigh when we think what we might have been? Why is every one of us missing his highest? Why are we all shut out from our trees of life? There is one word, one universal word, that tells the sad story for us all. It is selfishness — selfishness from the beginning. If we had not been selfish, if we had lived for God from the beginning, if we had been consecrated, we know it would have been different; we should have had our Eden inside and not outside; we should have eaten in God's due time of our tree of life, and have come to what He made us for — our fullest and our best life.

And then add to this sense of exclusion, this consciousness of having missed our best, the other symbol of the cherubims. What is it that keeps us from our tree of life today? What is it that, when we have once lost it, keeps us shut out from the dream and pattern of our existence? Behold, it is those very forces, those same circumstances which ought to and which might have taken our hands and been our guides, to lead us to our highest possibilities. If you are a student who scoffs and is irreverent, what has made you so? That very study, that very science, which might have led you to a profound and thoughtful and tender awe of God. Or you are a working man or a working woman, and your work has made you bitter and discontented, that very work which was sent to make you happy and healthy. Or you have lived a life of society and you have grown frivolous and selfish by that contact with your fellow-men which might have made you earnest and self-forgetful. Or you have been rich, and your riches have made you proud instead of humble. These are the powers which ought to make us good, and do so

often make us bad; whose mission is to bring men's souls to God and
to their own best attainment, but which our obstinacy so often com-
pels to stand between us and God, and shut us out from Him. These
are the cherubims with flaming swords that keep us from our tree of
life.

I cannot set before you as I wish I could that universal tragedy of
human existence — the consciousness of every man living that he has
not found his best. I can only rely on what I know is in the heart of every one of you giving confirmation to my words. The lost tree of life!
we were driven out from it before we tasted it, and we have lived in exile
from it all our days, the most successful and the most unfortunate of
us alike. How little is the difference of our success or our misfortune,
after all! we have all together failed of the best that we were made for,
failed of the fulness of our life.

So true is the beginning of the Bible to our continual life! so in our
own experience we find the everlasting warrant of that much-disputed
tale of Genesis! But, thank God! the end of the Bible is just as true. As
true as this universal fact of all men's failure is the other fact, that no
man's failure is final or necessarily fatal; that every man's lost tree of
life is kept by God, and that he may find it again in God's Paradise if he
comes there in humble consecration.

Let us put figures and allegories aside for a moment. The truth of
Christianity is this: that however a man has failed by his selfishness of
the fulness of life for which God made him, the moment that, led by
the love of Christ, he casts his selfishness aside and consecrates himself
to God, that lost possibility reappears; he begins to realize and attempt
again in hope the highest idea of his life; the faded colors brighten; the
crowding walls open and disappear. This is the deepest, noblest Christian consciousness. Very far off, very dimly seen as yet, hoped-for not by
any struggle of its own but by the gift of the Mercy and Power to which
it is now given, the soul that is in God believes in its own perfectibility,
and dares to set itself perfection as the mark of life, short of which it
cannot rest satisfied.

And when this change has come, when a soul has dared again to
realize and desire the life for which God made it, then also comes the
other change. The hindrances change back again to their true purpose

and are once more the helpers. That, too, is a most noble part of the Christian's experience, and one which every Christian recognizes. You prayed to God when you became His servant that He would take your enemies away, that He would free you from those circumstances which had hindered you from living a good life. But He did something better than what you prayed for. As you looked at your old enemies they did not disappear, but their old faces altered. You saw them still, but you saw them now changed into His servants. The business that had made you worldly stretched out new hands, all heavy with the gifts of charity. The nature which had stood like a wall between you and the truth of a Personal Creator, opened now a hundred voices all declaring Him. The men who had tempted you to pride and passion, all came with their opportunities of humility and patience. Everything was altered when you were altered. The cherubims had left their hostile guard above the gate, and now stood inviting you to let them lead you to the tree of life. This is the Fall supplanted by the Redemption. This completes the whole Bible of a human life.

This, then, is the truth of the tree of life, its loss and its recovery. We turn to the only human life in which it was never lost, the life of Jesus Christ. We own in Him the perfection of humanity — every human power at its best used for its best. With Him there was none of this brooding dissatisfaction that there is with us. Many a time His hard and heavy work weighed on Him, and once He cried to be released; but never is there any word of bitter regret as He looks back, never in all the Gospel one self-reproach that He had fallen short of completeness either in character or work. Oh, below all the pain, what a satisfaction there must have been in that tried and tortured heart! Who would not feel that any pain were easy if one could be as free as Jesus Christ was from self-reproach, if one could say as He said, "I have finished the work that thou gavest me to do," and at last, with one more "It is finished," lay a life that had completely succeeded back into the Father's hand?

Yes, Christ always lived to His fullest, and as we read His story we know why. The secret is not hard to find. It is in that one clear power of consecration that runs through all His life. It is because He is living to God from the beginning to the end that He lives so completely. And where His obedience is most manifest, the completeness of His life is most manifest, too. We see that in the Cross. He was never so alive as when He was dying there. There, where He reached the consummate obedience, He reached the consummation of life, too. The Being most alive, the Being whose life is running out into most vast and stupendous consequences, is He who hangs expiring there. The Cross is His Tree of Life.

And so with us, my friends. If we do really give ourselves to God, whatever cross that consecration brings us to will be our tree of life. It may seem as if, in making ourselves His, we strip our lives of their richness; we give up friends, we give up amusements, we give up easy days, we give up our own will to be the Lord's. It looks like death. It looks like emptying the precious wine of life away, and breaking the precious vase that held it. But as you go on in your sacrifice, behold! the memory of Eden is revived, and the prophecy of Paradise is fulfilled. The cross on which you stretch yourself sends its strength and abundance into you; and it is not dying, but living. No matter what men call it, you know that it is living. Your cross is your tree of life.

And yet again, the Cross of Christ may be not merely His Tree of Life, but ours. If it imparts its power to us; if, loving Him because He died upon it, we grow eager to give ourselves to Him and to our brethren; then that old wood on which they crucified Him becomes the source and fountain of our life. It is not merely that He never was more alive than when He hung there, but our life also is revived when we come nearest to it. The power of our self-sacrifices is in that self-sacrifice of His. Our crosses are cut out of that one inexhaustible Cross of Calvary.

Behold, then, for every man there are not two, there are three trees of life — the tree in Eden, the tree on Calvary, and the tree in the Paradise of God. For every man there is God's first design, and there is God's final salvation; but between the two there is Christ's Redemption. We lose our life; we find it in our Savior; we keep it unto life eternal.

Where do we all stand? Behind us is the loss; we have sinned and come short of the glory of God. Have we recovered our life at the Cross? If we have, then, by obedience springing out of gratitude, the way is open for us into the eternal life of God. "Blessed are they that do his commandments," that they may have a right to the tree of life, and enter in through the gates into the city.

A preacher of righteousness and hope
Majestic in stature
Impetuous in utterance
Rejoicing in the truth

Unhampered by the bonds of Church or station
He brought by his life and doctrine
Fresh faith to a people
Fresh meaning to ancient creeds

*from an inscription at the*
*Phillips Brooks House,*
*Harvard University*